DREAM

THE REAL WINDOWS TO YOUR LIFE

DREAMS

THE REAL WINDOWS TO YOUR LIFE

Rhondda Stewart-Garfield

Kangaroo Press

Dedicated
to you with love

Cover design by Darian Causby
using a photograph by
Jim Frazier

Reprinted in paperback 1994
First published in 1993 by Kangaroo Press Pty Ltd
3 Whitehall Road Kenthurst NSW 2156 Australia
P.O. Box 6125 Dural Delivery Centre NSW 2158 Australia
Typeset by G.T. Setters Pty Limited
Printed in Hong Kong through Colorcraft Ltd

ISBN 0 86417 626 0

Contents

Acknowledgments

I would like to express my profound appreciation and thanks to my husband Frank, who firstly talked me into writing this book and secondly spent hours in pre-editing and offering suggestions, to thank my daughter Catherine for being so patient and forgiving while I was consumed by writing it, Jacki McFarlane for typing the rough drafts while offering support and enthusiasm, and Sue Bishop for the illustrations. I would also like to give a special thanks to a special friend, Adam Nichols, for his assistance and support.

Foreword

When it comes to presenting her credentials, which are considerable, Rhondda is more than well qualified to speak for herself. I'm here to speak as her friend. Although she credits me with being her mentor, I really did little more than help her to learn her ABCs. The credit for what she has achieved since then is entirely her own.

From the moment she first stepped through my door, it wasn't difficult to see that there was something special about Rhondda. There is a quality about her that glows, and it is more than her aura. She may have learned with me but she has never really been my student. From the very start she has been a loving spirit-sister. She outgrew the modest dimensions of those early classes very quickly, but I've been blessed with her friendship ever since. Whenever I am in need of help and advice, Rhondda is one of the first two people I will call. That is, if she doesn't call me first, to say, 'I keep thinking about you, is there something you need?' Seriously, it happens!

I place a high value on my own integrity so I don't make recommendations lightly, but words cannot recommend Rhondda highly enough.

Dawn Shelley Thomas

[*Editor's Note:* Formerly known as Dawn Hill, Dawn has remarried and is now known as Dawn Shelley Thomas. She is the author of *Edge of Reality* (1987), and *Reaching for the Other Side* (1982), Pan Books (Australia) Pty Ltd.]

Introduction

I have been involved in the field of the parapsychology for over twenty years. Parapsychology is the study of the paranormal, the unknown, that which is beyond our normal reality and into the level of awareness known as the psyche, psychic perception or the sixth sense. At this level of awareness all our senses are fully operable, and accept the existence of the spirit forces or energy fields that surround the physical body. The energy field that exists around all living things is called the aura or auric field.

The adept or psychic can read the aura, within which is stored a memory of the individual's life. If you are able to see, feel and relate to a person's aura, you can perceive clairvoyantly what has happened to that person in the past, what is happening in the present and what will happen in the future, as well as their current state of physical health.

As a small child I found I was very sensitive to the auric fields of friends and family: I received a lot of personal information about them and before long realised I was able to read their futures. This all came about from an experience I had when I was nine years old. I was rushed to hospital with a suspected ruptured appendix, at the same time having been diagnosed with hepatitis. During surgery my body went into distress and I was pronounced clinically dead. While the doctors were trying to revive me I had an out-of-body experience and opened the door of clairvoyance in my mind. I suddenly had a psychic awareness of the spirit realms which enabled me to communicate with them. Leaving my physical body I travelled into another dimension, outside what we know as our physical existence, to a place where spirits exist—the astral plane. (In our unaware state we live in the physical level of existence, but beyond this exists the astral plane, also referred to as the fourth dimension.) I started communicating with 'guides', spirits which exist in the astral planes and work with us to help us with our physical existence and guide us with the clairvoyant aspects of our life.

I returned to my body as it responded to the doctors' efforts and awakened later to the realisation that I had opened my channel to clairvoyance. Over the years I gradually built up an understanding of my sensitivity and expanded my abilities.

After many years of uncertainty about how to use my clairvoyant abilities, I had the good fortune to meet Dawn Hill[1], who became my very close friend and mentor and helped direct my awareness. I started working with my psychic skills, seeing people who wanted me to look into their futures to see where their lives were going. I used the clairvoyant channel, communicating with my spirit guides who told me what choices these people had to make in their lives. Often people would be unaware that they had more than one option, and it benefited them to know they had more control over their destinies than they had thought. This opened their awareness of their potential, allowing them to look at situations more objectively. I call this process a 'forecast of potential direction'. It is accomplished through an auric reading or through psychometry (reading the energy of the aura through jewellery or objects that belong to the person).

I also became very involved in counselling clients who needed help with low self-esteem. I started teaching the application of positive thinking through self-development classes, teaching people to open their perceptions and to develop communication skills with their guides in the astral plane. I taught techniques of meditation during the class, working on the rediscovery of all the parts of oneself, slowly opening the sixth sense, which can be described as a hypersensitivity to the other five senses. Through applied techiques and exercises my clients slowly opened to their own guides and psychic abilities in the same way I had opened to my own.

Working with clients and students, I became aware that many of them talked about their dreams. Sometimes when they discussed issues they were trying to resolve I would ask what kind of dreams they were currently having. Dreams kept coming up as an item that had to be looked at as integral to a person's totality. Their emotions, their physical health, their pasts and their futures were inexorably linked to their dream structure.

After many years of communicating with different guides at increasing levels of complexity, I met my 'higher self' (or 'personal teacher'), whom I call Thomas. The higher self is the highest level of personal guidance that we normally contact in the astral, our 'true teacher' from the astral plane. The guides who exist at

---

[1]Dawn Hill: *Edge of Reality* (1987), and *Reaching for the Other Side* (1982), Pan Books Australia Pty Ltd

lower levels in the astral, who teach us and open our awareness, are receiving their understanding and communication from the higher self. We could liken the higher self to the managing director of a company, the guides to the managers and ourselves to the workers, living out the reality of life in the physical plane but receiving direction and assistance from the astral plane. Despite this, we are still the masters of our own destiny. The guides and our higher selves do not want to live our lives for us, but instead wish to guide and help us like a parent, allowing us to make the choices we have to make ourselves. They are there merely to support and love us whatever we choose to do in life.

There are many levels of teachers beyond the personal teacher or higher self, spirits who work with many aspects of understanding and can teach us a great deal about any subject matter. Through Thomas I contacted such beings when I started seeing the need to better understand my clients' dreams; in doing this I was trained from the astral level in dream interpretation. Over the years the desire grew to create not just an understanding for me but also for my clients, and I started accumulating knowledge and data, putting it together to formulate a commonsense approach to allow people to look at their dreams and empower themselves in their awakened state to create balance and resolve in their lives.

Thomas spent many years training me in a broader comprehension of the astral plane to better understand energy and what the aura is, as well as introducing me to many other teachers who have skilled me in all aspects of the psychic field. My time over the last few years has been spent accumulating a great deal of knowledge and understanding of the field of dreams.

The meditation exercises that Thomas gave me greatly assisted my students with their awareness development and with their skills in communicating with their guides and higher selves. The exercises enabled me to understand their dreams and to help them interpret their dreams themselves. I gave my students other exercises which helped them extend and open their awareness of the auric field and their dream symbolism. Dawn Hill was referring to me people interested in developing their psychic potential, people who either had had experiences they could not understand and wanted to know more or who just had an interest in their personal development. So it was that I started teaching—and some ten years later I am still teaching.

We all have the ability to develop our psychic awareness and the ability to further the understanding of our dreams; we all have the potential to work with healing using the aura. All manner of physical and emotional maladies are clearly and accurately reflected in the aura. Injury, illness and emotional trauma can be seen in the colour and energy level of the aura, much as a doctor uses an x-ray or CAT-scan.

I use colour therapy in conjunction with examining the aura in diagnosing and healing. Colour therapy is the use of a continuous flow of healing energy from the astral plane which is magnified down to our physical plane and channelled through us to work on balancing an aura, aligning the chakra centres and the pitch or vibration of the auric field. Much in the same way a piano tuner adjusts the pitch of each key on the piano, the clairvoyant can adjust the energy frequency of each chakra centre to balance the colour and vibrational frequency of the aura, which affects our dream patterns. Working with colour therapy is also something I teach my students. These topics are covered in the chapter on colour and dreaming (page 79). Barbara Ann Brennan's book on colour therapy, *Hands of Light*[2], is excellent for those wishing to read further.

Two years ago I was greeted by a spirit known as the Chohan, who works with a healing council in the astral. He opened my awareness to the 'karmic blueprint', an accumulation of memories from past-life experiences mapped out with our new direction in life for our future incarnation. I now had another tool to use in dream management analysis. Our karmic blueprint forecasts the development of our present physical life. It gives us tools to work with through having an innate, cellular memory of who we have been and what we have done in past lives. It helps us re-awaken previously-used talents relevant to present potentials in this life-focus. Prior to conception we can limit or block our true potential or our awareness of past-life talents, which may lead us to have the feeling we are continually going around in circles. Through working with the Chohan I am able to clear these restrictions and blocks, thus opening the blueprint to its full potential free of self-imposed restrictions and past-life traumas. I can also access traumas that have been relayed from 'parallel structures', such as twin souls or soulmates at the astral level.

Let me explain this: Some of us may have come from the same 'over-soul', which is like having the same mother, or from a separate over-soul, which is like having a neighbour with exactly the same interests and understanding of life as oneself. In our physical plane this gives us strong connections with each other as we parallel our experiences back and forth. Simply put, we can live through emotions that belong to another person (who may exist in either this lifetime or another) and accept them as our own. Your dream patterns would show this

---

[2]Barbara Ann Brennan: *Hands of Light* (1987), Bantam Books, USA

quite clearly. Through working with the Chohan I can clear the restrictions, which are not our own, which we have taken on.

Being able to analyse your own dreams will allow you to clear many of the restrictions imposed upon you. These restrictions show up as past-life memories we have brought through into our present awareness at a cellular memory-level from birth, past-life memories that are disruptive to our life-focus and direction. This book will help you learn the process to release them, thus enhancing or opening your awareness without restrictions. I was moved to write it because I wanted to share my discovery of the ability we all have to interpret our own dreams. I wanted to create a book that everyone could read, whether they were esoterically aware or not. It is a handbook for self-interpretation of your own dreams. To do this it takes you into a number of areas which on the surface may seem unrelated; but as you read on you will appreciate their relevance.

Before You Begin

Some people pick up a book and read it from beginning to end without skipping a page. Some people like to get to the 'meat and potatoes' straight away and skip over the contents, introduction, foreword, and so on. Some people like to look at the last page for a sneak preview of how things come out in the end.

I've tried to accommodate each of these styles of reading so feel free to begin with the last page. Start by recording your dreams in the journal provided in the back of the book—or go straight to the chapter called Types of Dreams and learn how to classify yours—start at the front and learn some of the background first before you get into the book in depth. You'll probably read it several times through anyway as it makes a great bedside companion.

CHAPTER 1

An Introduction to Dream Awakening

From the moment you open your eyes in the morning until you close them at night your mind, both consciously and subconsciously, is recording data. Everything you see, smell, taste, touch and hear is recorded. You activate and store the plans you are making for the day. You look at your work schedule, at the problems and situations coming up, and you absorb and memorise those factors.

You could be driving home from work and witness a car accident or be involved in one. At the conscious level you deal with all the factors—you ring the police, you take care of yourself and the car. You do everything that can be done and you go home.

At night, in your dream state, your mind processes and analyses what happened. If you have resolved the accident you may merely release some anger in the dream state, the final stage of the process. This means you have actually processed and cleared the situation out of the subconscious level into the conscious level of awareness in your dream state.

If the accident has stirred up emotions that are not resolved your mind moves them down into the subconscious where they are stored, the initial stage of the data or experience collection. 'Files' (from the Akashic records—*see* Glossary, p. 142) that already exist are opened and the new information compared to their data. The new information is allocated either to an existing file or to a new file created for it.

Repeatedly over the next twenty-one day cycle you have the opportunity of reviewing the files at this level through your dreaming. If you still do not resolve your feelings, your emotions or the situation, the trauma deepens and is moved and stored at a deeper level. At this deeper level, if it remains unresolved, the only way to access the trauma at a later date will be through hypnosis or through the keys that I introduce to you later in the book. Left unresolved such a trauma may manifest itself later through a phobia, a reaction to a normally non-stressful event in which you feel extreme anxiety. The phobia is not usually related to the situation you are actually in. In the case of the accident it could be triggered by stopping at a set of traffic lights, for instance. Your memory of the accident and the trauma attached to it will be triggered each time you stop at a red traffic light.

Nightmares are directly related to deep-seated traumas that have not been resolved. For example, your sister might have been injured in the car accident and you did not attend to her injury for one reason or another. Your dreams might show her being in danger and you chasing after her but unable to get to her, or your sister crying for help, and you reaching out toward her and then waking up, quite startled, to realise that you neglected her when she needed you. The dream may become progressively more bizarre on successive nights. This particular type of nightmare would be resolved by phoning your sister, the person in your thoughts, and seeing how she is; reassuring yourself of her well-being would clear the sequence of the nightmare in your dream pattern.

Sleep levels

Technically, as measured by an EEG, there are four sleep levels, defined by different levels of brain wave activity, plus one called REM (rapid eye movement) sleep, and the awakened state:[3]

Level 0 (the awakened state)   = Beta
Level 1   = Alpha
Level 2   = Theta
Levels 3 and 4 (deep sleep levels) = Delta

The different types of brain waves in each state are diagrammatically represented in the graph.

Beta brain waves are measured at 15 to 30 vibrations (hertz or Hz) per second. They have the highest frequency or number of waves per second but lowest amplitude (height) of wave action. Beta waves represent normal brain activity while awake.

[3]Atkinson, Atkinson, Smith, Hilgard: *Introduction to Psychology*, 9th ed. (1987), HBJ College Publications, New York

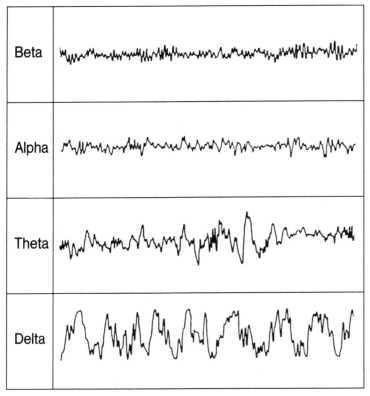

Beta	
Alpha	
Theta	
Delta	

Brain waves
measured by EEG

Alpha brain waves, at 8 to 12 Hz, occur in that very relaxed state between being awake and being asleep, or in very light sleep. This is also the state where REM (rapid eye movement) dreaming occurs, at roughly 90-minute intervals. (Some sources differentiate between Alpha and REM, creating a fifth EEG or sleep pattern in which the brain waves are the same as alpha waves but with the addition of eye movement.) While adults stay in REM for 20 minutes of each 90-minute sleep cycle, or about 20% of the time, children up to the age of 12 tend to stay in REM for 50–80% of this time. The average adult would go through five REM periods per night[4].

There is some evidence that maximal psychological restoration of the mind takes place during these REM periods. Women frequently have longer REM periods during their pre-menstrual phase, a time characterised by irritability, depression, and anxiety (Hartman, 1984). This would explain why women may

[4] Plotnik, R. & Mollenauer, S.: *Brain & Behaviour* (1978), Harper & Row, New York

experience during the pre-menstrual period not only more dream activity but disturbed and irrational ones as well.

Theta brain waves, at 5 to 7 Hz, occur in deep sleep. A common characteristic of this state is intermittent 'spindles' or rapid bursts of activity of high frequency but low amplitude.

Delta brain waves, at 2 to 4 Hz, show the lowest wave frequency per second but highest amplitude or height of wave action. They occur in the deeper level of sleep. Male athletes on a heavy training schedule tend to stay in the deeper levels of sleep longer, which suggests maximal physical restoration during this period. There are actually two levels of delta. I believe that physical restoration takes place on the first level while astral travel may take place during the second or deeper level.

What we are seeing here is that a person does not just fall asleep and awaken eight hours later; instead going through a series of 90-minute intervals alternating between physical and mental restoration and astral travel. Since the sleep pattern begins by going down fairly quickly to the delta level without an REM period, it seems logical to postulate that a delta level, gathering data, followed by a theta to correlate data, is necessary to set things up for the next REM period.

It is interesting to note here that the brain never sleeps. In fact it functions much like a personal computer. With a PC the data is entered very slowly, between 20–100 words per minute, depending on the typing skill of the operator. The data inside the computer is sorted, scanned, analysed, et cetera, at roughly the speed of light. The human brain enters data at a relatively slow pace through the five senses. During the deeper sleep levels (theta) the brain analyses, sorts and compares data entered today with data stored previously.

Where unresolved issues come up during the processing of the data, your subconscious can structure a dream which can replay those same issues, but in a different scenario, which may aid their final solution. If the issue is one based in the future, such as finding a mate, your subconscious may set up a preliminary meeting with a potential mate, or even with someone you knew in a past life, on the astral level (more on that later). Sometimes when the issue is current but similar to something resolved in a past life, your 'chakras' (see Glossary, p.143) may pull information from the 'fohatic pool' or 'Akashic records' (see Glossary, p.142) of your past lives to give you the resolution you seek currently. This information is also replayed to you during the dream state and stored in the subconscious at the solar plexus chakra. (See Appendix C, p.133, for detailed information on chakra centres.)

The auric field

Why is the auric field relevant to dreams?

All of our life experiences, which are played back to us in dreams, are stored in the aura. What exactly is an aura? An aura is an energy field, a scientifically measurable, physical energy field that surrounds the body.

Where does the aura come from?

We have seven major energy centres within the body called chakra centres. All of the colours of the spectrum are represented in each chakra, but there is one dominant colour in each centre. The base chakra is red in appearance, the spleen chakra is orange, solar plexus yellow, heart chakra green, throat chakra blue, brow or third eye chakra indigo and the crown chakra violet.

The colours from each chakra radiate outward to form the auric field surrounding the physical body. If we're healthy and fit, we radiate a current of energy that exhibits a lovely glow of light and energy around the body. If we're suffering a health condition or we're going through a problem, a dull, dark colour will dominate the aura. We can emotionally block our chakra centres, causing energy restriction; if we don't resolve the problem, we can manifest not only a physical illness but nightmares as well. The emotions that cause centres to be blocked are those of negativity, including fear, shock, anger, jealousy, hate. The chakra centres breathe—they breathe energy—and the current of energy they breathe promotes health in that part of the body. That's why each of the chakra centres is so important. Each one radiates out an energy field that works in harmony with the body to create health and balance.

The health status of an individual can be reviewed by evaluating the aura. By looking at the aura we gain a perception or understanding of the problems people are dealing with. The aura is a very important part of our existence because it is the focus of our physical energy. We can utilise our awareness of chakra centres to keep them clear and functional; by doing this we keep ourselves clear and functional. We stabilise in our direction in life by keeping our physical energy at its highest peak of performance.

People ask, 'What colour is your aura? What colour is mine?' The aura changes colour continuously, depending on what we are feeling or thinking at that moment. We do have a dominant colour according to our mood and our state of health. If I was feeling happy I would be radiating a lovely green or blue. If I was perhaps very jealous or angry I could radiate a very dark green for envy, jealousy or pure frustration.

Why do we have an aura? How does the aura form? When we incarnate (make the transition from a spirit body to a physical body) we leave 'formats of energy' through the seven levels of the astral. Each level of energy is called an astral body. Each astral body has a vibration or a pitch of energy related to one of the colours of the spectrum: (ROY G BIV)—Red, Orange, Yellow, Green, Blue, Indigo, Violet). These formats of energy are stored data collected from all our past-life experiences, information that we are going to need to assist us with this life incarnation. The formats align with our major chakras. The base centre, red in frequency, has an astral body red in frequency; the spleen, orange astral body frequency; solar plexus, yellow; heart, green; throat, blue; brow (third eye), indigo; and the crown centre, violet, aligns with the seventh astral body.

The fohatic energy field creates a vibrational energy field (the aura) that continuously feeds us the data appropriate to the various times in our lives. Memories of past-life experiences which exist at a cellular level assist us with similar experiences in this lifetime. These memories are sometimes accessed through the subconscious during the dream state. We also relay current data (current daily life experiences, thoughts, pleasures and traumas) back to our astral bodies. After our physical body dies, our spiritual body, an etheric field of energy (the soul) separates from it. All the data stored in the energy centres are at this point relayed back to the astral bodies as we go through a process called the 'death sequence', in which the soul or etheric body leaves our physical body and returns to the etheric level of existence in the astral plane. The astral bodies connect with each other and go back to the fohatic pool (*see* Glossary, p.143) where the awareness of our existence originates. All knowledge exists within the fohatic energy field, also known as the Akashic record—all souls exist on the periphery of that energy. When we decide to incarnate we move within the flow and align with the data of past-life experiences. A body of spirits that I call the Pre-birth Council aligns us with all the data that we need for this lifetime; at the point of reincarnation, as we descend, our astral bodies are left at the appropriate levels of the astral with the stored information which they relay to us through our chakra centres as necessary throughout life.

At the time of death, the soul goes back to the fohatic energy field and the new information it has accumulated is absorbed into the awareness of that energy. The formats of energy that we call 'astral bodies' are also filed into fohatic energy and become part of the collective thought of existence. The knowledge of everything that has ever been or is now or ever will be in the future exists in this fohatic energy field.

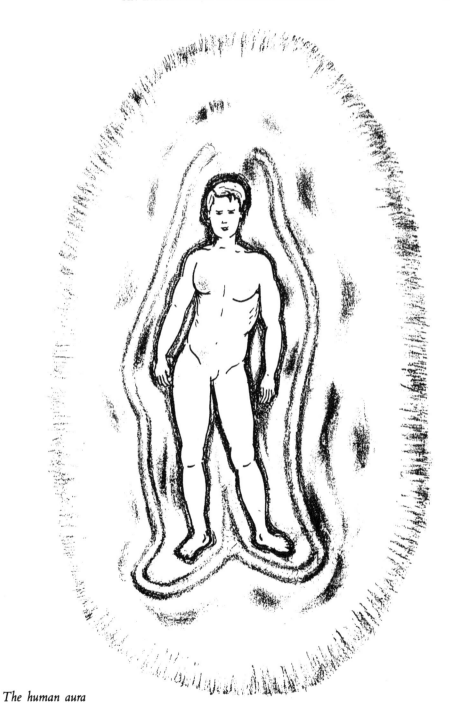

The human aura

The aura is made up of seven major energy centres that radiate out and form an energy field around us. The continual relaying of data backward and forward from the physical to the astral planes, where our astral bodies are, is also a cleansing process. Energy centres breathe and live and experience as we do. They absorb all data relevant to us.

Beyond the physical auric field we have an etheric energy field, an auric field that extends itself beyond what we are as a physical being. Because we are both a physical being—a collection of inanimate chemical elements in the body form— and a spirit being, which gives life to the physical form, we have different levels to our aura. The level that we perceive when we look at an aura is the physical level. There are physical boundaries beyond those which relate purely to our spirit force. The level of the aura beyond the physical works on the cleaning process of the physical to keep energy levels vitalised so the body is functioning at its peak.

The astral bodies existing at different levels are affected by our life experiences. At times we become out of alignment with our astral bodies, usually when we have gone through some emotional experience which has literally 'blown out' the astral body. When this happens we feel very disorientated and disconnected from ourselves. At these times we are normally drawn to a park or have a need to work in the garden, where the influence of nature helps us to realign the physical body with the astral bodies.

How is this relevant to the dream state?

Sometimes, when you are sleeping, your etheric body leaves your physical body to travel through the astral. You can encounter other people in your dream state and you can also align with their astral bodies. This can create very confusing situations. If you allow someone else's astral bodies into your space, something like a collision can take place. If you are going through a problem with a particular person at that moment in your life, you may start dreaming about it. You do this in an attempt to resolve whatever crisis you have in the physical, but at times you entangle your astral bodies and instead of resolving the problem, it gets worse. You feel overwhelmed by the person because they are in your space or you are in theirs.

Affirmations repeated in the morning when you awaken and are starting your day help clear out and release entangled astral bodies. Affirm that, 'I wish to disassociate at every level of my existence from any energy that belongs to other people. I ask that my astral bodies are cleaned and aligned purely with me and I release any energies that are attached to other people.'

Chakra centres are very relevant to our dreams. When we go through trauma, the data is processed through the chakra centres. At times our emotions block our chakra centres—when we are overwhelmed by feelings of unhappiness, uncertainty, or confused about which direction to take. Blocks in our energy centres restrict us in our physical lives because they actually deplete our physical energy level, as well as slowing down access and retrieval from the astral bodies. We can start having very abstract dreams that make no sense at all. The signs to watch for are:

1. Being aware that something in your life is not functioning properly.
2. Bouts of tiredness, anxiety, concern and confusion are a sign of a blocked chakra centre disrupting an astral body. This disrupts your dream status as well as your physical health and well-being.

Chakra centres in balance are reflected by our current state of physical energy. Feeling healthy and full of vitality, both mentally and physically, are good signs that there are no blockages in the chakras and that they are breathing well. If they are out of balance or blocked then we have an imbalance in our energy flow that will cause disruptions at all levels that we exist in, especially at our dream state level.

Reincarnation

What does reincarnation have to do with dreaming? I've included this section to give you some insight into those seemingly inexplicable dreams which involve a past life, and those which generate feelings of *déjà vu*.

All souls exist in the fohatic energy field (or the energy of existence). You exist on the periphery of this energy. Within the energy is the data or memory of every experience you've had and every other soul has had since long before the beginning of time. Past-life experiences are recorded in this flow of energy.

When you as a soul decide to incarnate, the soul realigns with the flow of energy. It goes into the flow and collects all the data and memory that it needs to carry it forward into this lifetime. You project forward an awareness of what you wish to achieve in your new incarnation and the 'blueprint' which outlines your life's purpose is formed. You decide this when you are on the periphery, with your focus on where you're going and what you choose to have in your life path. You move into the flow and current of energy and slowly collect all the memory and data.

The imprint of the astral bodies as the soul descends through the fohatic pool into the physical realm

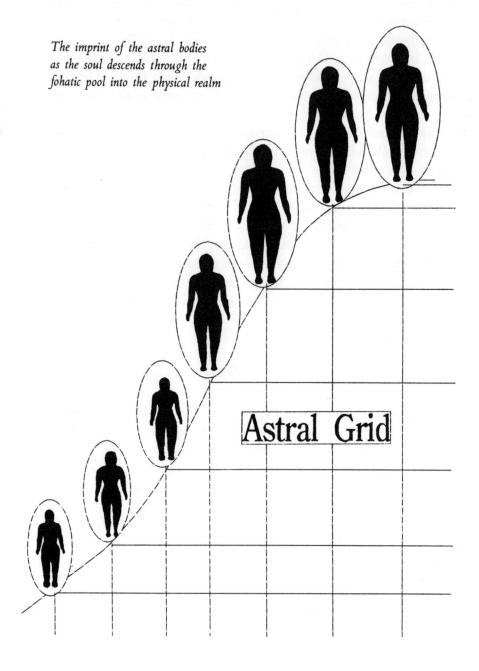

Astral Grid

You start a descent into alignment with being born. You choose your parents or you choose a collection of people who would suit you as a parent, you align with them and the most appropriate situations in the physical world. When you align properly with your prospective parents, you start the transition of birth from your etheric level of existence. As you descend through the astral you deposit formats of energy (astral bodies) which are the collection of your total memory, the data of all your past-life experiences plus the current direction in life. Your astral bodies project the information and data down into your physical form.

As the foetus develops in the mother's womb it develops the seven primary centres of energy or chakra centres. The information from the astral bodies is relayed through these chakra centres, which begin to collect and store all the information relevant to your current life path, in other words, the information relevant to what you're going to be achieving in this lifetime. The programming of this information is relayed through each centre in the body. The preordained structure of your existence (dictated by your DNA), e.g. the colour of your hair, height, body build, behaviour patterns, health status, is all relayed into your chakra centres, stored and expanded as you develop and grow, until you go through the transition of being physically born. An angel sent by the Pre-birth Council forms a protective shell around mother and baby. There is also a fohatic cord which connects the fohatic energy field, the energy of existence, to your mother and your physical form. There is a lovely seal of gold around this connection which provides protection during your descent into life.

After you're born the protective shell remains around you for the first three months of your life. This is because you're still forming your chakra centres. Eventually the vibration of the centres forms a lovely ray, an aura, around the physical form. 'Elementals' or little 'devic spirits' (see Glossary, p.143) come forward and actually vibrate the shell. If the pitch under the shell is perfect and each centre is fully developed and functional, they tap the shell, it vibrates inside and the shell cracks. A beautiful rainbow of light, a fully formed aura, then forms around you. Your chakra centres start breathing, focusing and keeping the balance of energy flowing through the body.

Realigned with your astral bodies, you're now in a position to retrieve all necessary memory and data from past-life experiences. This information, which was collectively stored in your astral bodies, is brought back into your current life to help with your experiences and expansion.

Prior to birth, in the nine months that your mother is pregnant, your soul moves back and forth from the uterus to the plane in which you existed before birth. At the time of birth, or very close to it, the soul aligns with the physical body and goes through the birth process. When this happens you lose the memory of previous physical and spiritual incarnations, due to the alignment of one of the astral bodies between your physical and your etheric body (or soul). The astral body acts as a filter to screen the flow of information between the physical and the etheric planes. The trauma of birth erases the conscious memory of where you have been and aligns you with the present. You start adapting and acclimatising to the environment you are now in, slowly adjusting to your new environment as you grow.

A soul makes the decision to incarnate to resolve old karma as well as to learn and experience physical life. Reincarnation is something we have all done before. We have all had many lifetimes. This present one is the level we are now working on.

Dream lovers

If you are single and free, and would like to form a relationship in your physical life, you can expand that desire into your sleep state and your astral projection. While in the astral plane you can actually extend an emotional vibration that draws in and attracts other souls also looking for a relationship. (I met my husband Frank this way.)

If you acknowledge in your dream state or out-of-body state that you have successfully attracted another being at another level, in your awakened state you can then affirm the connection with that person on the physical plane. It can be a very beneficial and fulfilling life experience.

If the astral projection demonstrates an experience with someone you know, dreaming about a feeling of love moving between the two of you may open up a relationship in the physical in your awakened state. If it is someone you don't know currently but meet in the astral, you feel very attracted and experience a time of travelling together through the astral. Feelings of love expanding and opening between you may draw this person toward you in your awakened state in your physical life. When that person appears you feel very drawn to them—as if you've known them before and had a connection with them before. As the relationship develops a lot of things that you experience together in the physical will be familiar *(déjà vu)* as they will have happened previously in the astral plane as a 'preview of coming attractions'.

You can create a dream lover, actually manifesting the perfect person in your life. Affirm when you go to sleep that when you leave your body you will actually go searching to attract your soulmate, someone you're going to share your life with in the physical. On returning to the physical plane we can draw those influences into our lives and can have very meaningful relationships with our dream lovers.

Two words of caution here:

1. Be sure you *completely* define the mate you're looking for. If you ask for someone who is very good looking and a sex maniac, you may receive just that! Your life could be miserable from then on, due to incompatible personal habits, attitudes, untidiness, BO.

2. Sometimes we go into conflict with our feelings. We may dream about having a relationship with someone we work with or know and yet have a very tempestuous type of relationship with them in the physical where we just can't seem to get on. It may be because we are putting too much expectation into our feelings which are not being recognised in the physical; in a way we're taking it out on the person or they are taking it out on us.

When we have had an out-of-body experience in the astral, we can come back feeling very much in love and happy. If this doesn't quickly become a reality it can make us feel very frustrated and angry, which can actually stop us from recognising that we are in a precognitive state, that we are looking forward at something we want to have happen here. If we relax and accept it as a statement of things to come (let it happen instead of 'pushing the river') then we will recognise the beings that we attract are right for us and our play in the astral will become our play in the physical.

In the astral we can also meet people we know in the physical with whom we have very difficult relationships. We may take our anger with us and actually extend it in our communication in the astral. Coming back into the physical and dealing with these people, we find they have a brick wall up already prepared; they are blocked from listening to us because they have done that already in the astral. You need a gentler approach. Realise that you have already pushed this person's back against a wall and that you're going to have to offer a hand of support or a little bit more emotion and caring before the wall will come down and you can communicate what you're feeling.

Because of your release in the astral you may feel very confident about what you have to say to them. But because you have released that anger they may feel very resentful or shut away from you. By offering a hand or an extension of feelings and relaxing them first, you'll pull the wall down and be able to resolve the situation in your awakened state.

You may also attract ex-lovers in your astral projection. You had a relationship that broke up six months ago and you haven't seen the person since but they have now appeared in your dream. It can be a very difficult time at first during your awakened state to deal with the return (in your dream) of someone that you have finished an experience with. Just because you are re-attracting them in the astral plane does not mean that you still have something to work through. All that may be required is an affirmation of acknowledgment that the relationship is now one of friendship. Accept that the relationship has ended and you are releasing it with love. If that person returns into your physical existence, you will have purely a friendship with no emotional attachments.

Astral bodies

Prior to birth we go through a process of aligning with the fohatic energy or 'Akashic records' which then forms a structure that becomes an integral part of our cellular memory of experiences from past lives and is imprinted in the DNA. It's only been in very recent years that scientists have 'discovered' (i.e. become aware of a truth that has always existed) that DNA is not just the blueprint of our physical structure but also of certain behaviour patterns or 'cell level memory'. We go through an alignment with this memory, which forms a format of energy that we bring into or align with in the physical plane.

How do we do this?

We align with our cellular memory through our chakra centres. Its energy and data are left at the seven levels of the astral in the formations of energy called astral bodies, which are the memory stores of all that we have experienced in prior lives. They relay that information to us at appropriate times in our lifetime through our chakra centres so that cellular memory is created.

Where or how does this influence our lives?

Every time we are about to experience something new we retrieve data from something that aligns with our new experience from our past-life experience.

For example, if we are about to take on a new career or are about to go and learn something new then we would align with data where we have perhaps gained knowledge in this type of skill before. Let's say we are looking at doing an art course. We would align with lifetimes where we have experienced perhaps being an artist or being associated with an artist. It would amplify the potential of what we could do now.

When we align with this data in the fohatic energy field we create a 'blueprint', a new structure of life that outlines all the new directions that we are choosing to take, including karma that we are working through (see Glossary, p.144), and what our lesson is, plus all the past-life experiences that are going to help us with this lifetime. All this information is relayed through our astral bodies into our chakra centres at the time that we need to experience it. We align with past experiences when we are attacking something new, which enhances the potential of what we can do. As we have an experience the memory or data of that experience is returned to the astral bodies to be retrieved at a later date and/or taken over to the fohatic energy field for storage.

When we go through an experience that causes us pain or anguish, or we go through an emotional crisis, the astral bodies move slightly out of alignment so they're not affected by our trauma. They store the memory but they are not affected by the actual trauma. When this happens we feel very disorientated, not quite in focus, an experience we've all had when we've been going through some problem. As we start to feel better about ourselves and we resolve the crisis then the astral bodies naturally move back into alignment with us and we start to feel whole and complete again. They are another part of our awareness.

When we sleep at night and project out of the physical, we align with our astral bodies; our astral bodies can subsequently align with those of loved ones or people we know. When this happens we can have recall of these out-of-body experiences. Sometimes we awake feeling very confused, as if we have met people and had this amazing dream that we just can't put together. The memory isn't quite there. Well, that is normally an indication of an out-of-body experience, of alignment with our astral bodies.

Our astral bodies are also affected by our health status. Going through a trauma which moves the astral bodies out of alignment can affect their energy. A person working with healing can cleanse and rebalance the astral bodies and bring them back into focus. If we start experiencing self-doubt or losing confidence in ourselves or we believe that we are not worthy of a situation, we can actually create an illness. Our astral bodies store the memory that we're choosing to be sick because we don't believe in ourselves or we don't believe in our abilities, or that we just feel we are unworthy of being healthy. The astral bodies accumulate that data, which can actually traumatise them to the degree that they relay the awareness of the trauma back to us in the physical, a situation which can amplify our sickness.

Any form of illness we go through is recorded in our astral bodies. We can develop subconscious fears about being sick and it's because we haven't resolved what we want ourselves and released the need to be sick.

On the other hand, many people have cured themselves of seemingly incurable diseases with positive thinking alone. Positive thinking works on clearing something out because you believe you should not hold on to it, that you are worthy of health and happiness, that you are worthy of having a healthy body structure. The use of affirmations can program the astral bodies and clear them naturally of health problems.

Working with energy can rebalance an alignment between the etheric being, the astral bodies and the soul. Through healing or working with colour therapy we can actually eliminate a lot of potential illness or we can bring illnesses that are working through the body to the stage where they are clearing out of the body, that is, we can bring an illness forward. Through healing we can actually eliminate, or reduce to a period of weeks or days, the effect of a situation that might otherwise have dragged on for months.

When we're in love with someone and they're not showing us the affection we want, our astral bodies align with their astral bodies and can become entangled, leading us to feel claustrophobic when people are close to us. This effect can occur with anyone—people you work with or people in your family structure. To release or detraumatise such a connection all you have to do is consciously repeat, 'I ask the creator to disentangle my astral bodies and release anyone I am entangled with and heal and rebalance my own astral bodies'. What that does is give breathing space to each person so you're back in your own space and not being made to feel claustrophobic.

Normally our desire to have something like love from someone else attracts the astral body of the person we're directing that love toward, our astral bodies become entangled and we feel a little confused about what's happening. Even worse, the other person can feel claustrophobic, which actually makes them feel the need to get away from us instead of getting closer to us. By clearing and just letting go of the astral bodies we're giving them their focus back, their freedom to feel and relate to us without a condition being placed on them.

Let's look at the astral body structure as a computer. Here we are, a mainframe being programmed with all the data we need for our lives, which is all coming from our asral bodies, giving us an awareness of what we want to do and where we want to go, as well of the past-life experiences that are going to help us with this transition or movement into life. If we block our potential then we are blocking ourselves and our awareness from our astral bodies so in a way we're not turning the computer on to receive the data. Through affirmation or just affirming that you care about yourself, you are choosing to direct yourself in life. You are realigning and tapping into that source of information and data.

CHAPTER 2

Types of Dreams

Dreams may be classified into one of three categories. The first type is what I call the subconscious dream, the second is past-life recall and the third covers out-of-body experiences.

How can you determine what type of dream you are having? Because you tend to forget the contents of a dream very soon after awakening, you should immediately record the dream on paper or on a small tape recorder kept next to your bed. Later in the day or at the end of the week you can recall your dreams to see which of the three categories each one fits into. Another technique helpful in remembering dreams is to make an affirmation just before bedtime that you wish to remember any dream occurring during the night. Affirm this to yourself and make an acknowledgment to yourself, 'I will remember my dreams, I choose to remember my dreams'. If you awaken after a dream, record it then and there, don't wait till the next morning.

Subconscious dreams

In the subconscious dream state we dream about our current problems. While asleep we actually receive all the data we need to resolve any life crisis that we are unable to deal with in a wakened state. This is not always obvious, however, for normally the dream is very abstract and you don't recognise what it is trying to tell you. The dream allows the playing out, through your imagination, of your wakened, conscious situations. Through the subconscious we explore an awareness of that which wasn't recognised on a conscious level. This type of dream is difficult to interpret because of the symbolism. For example, a dream in which you see yourself losing blood signifies a situation in which you are having difficulty making a choice in order to resolve a problem. Rehashing the problem over and over in your mind is draining your physical energy, thus the symbolism of losing blood is appropriate. Dreaming of performing on stage and receiving applause means that you are not being yourself but are behaving in a way that others want. If there is no-one in the theatre and you are alone, then you are letting yourself know that you are unhappy with a situation but want others to believe you agree with them or see the situation in the same way.

Falling in a dream is quite common and represents the feeling that you are out of control. Being exposed where others can see you in a communal or public shower or toilet represents the fact that your feelings are being hurt by others and that you are accepting the hurt without being confrontational. It also represents your inner vulnerability.

The eyes are the windows to the soul and from the time we awaken and open them we are viewing the world and the effects the world has on us: noises, sounds, confrontations from life and people. All of these are external influences that we absorb. The eyes record everything that has taken place in a day. All the data that the mind collects and accumulates is stored in the subconscious, including our activities and thoughts. When we go to bed and go to sleep, the subconscious is released from its restricted space and it becomes our conscious awareness in our sleep state. The subconscious awareness in the sleep state opens up all the experiences that we are and are not dealing with, running through all the different situations, all the different things we saw during the day, how people affected us, how we coped with different situations, what we saw as the day progressed. The mind places all this data into a format in the subconscious and then it releases during sleep, ticking over all the situations we've resolved or placed in a position of settlement or balance, and brings up the situations we haven't worked out.

This might include a situation where we had a disagreement with someone which we're still feeling very emotional about. We haven't resolved our feelings so our subconscious shows us this in a dream, which may be very abstract. We utilise symbolism and colour in such dreams, the mind bringing up a collective structure of images which appear in different colours. Sometimes the dream will be in very bright and vivid colours, at other times in basic black and white. Our subconscious does this so we are not frightened by whatever it is that distressed us during the day, showing it to us in a way that is not disruptive to our sleep. This is called a subconscious dream. In it we actually rethink a problem or a situation that we're not dealing with adequately in our everyday conscious state.

Most of the time we don't remember our subconscious dreams. We can actually say, 'I had a very full night dreaming but have no recall of it.' That means that we're not ready to remember or look at that situation. If we have a repetitive dream and eventually remember it, our subconscious is saying that there is a problem we should look at because we're confronted with it but not facing or dealing with it, perhaps on a daily basis.

A vivid colourful dream with panoramic views is actually a dream about a past-life experience. We normally dream about a past-life experience when we're involved in something of a similar nature in this lifetime. These dreams are normally very memorable and worth recording. By recording and looking at the present relevance of the dream, you realise that you have a better understanding of your current situation. We bring up past-life experiences in our dream state continuously because we have lived many lifetimes and we've done many things that we're striving to achieve again or work through again—talents that we've had in the past or potentials that we can utilise now. Our subconscious dreaming allows us to look at this and perhaps gain confidence in what we could achieve, what we are able to achieve now.

We dream in black and white when we are not one hundred per cent sure we want to know what the situation is. This represents a fear or reservation that we're bringing up in our dream state. We tend to remember our black and white dreaming because it's very simplistic and relevant to current issues in our lives. It would be the most focused dream-state closest to our normal reality without extreme levels of symbolism.

The subconscious is like a barometer, letting us know when something disturbs us. Some people call this gut level instinct. Gut level instinct is activated throughout the day as we experience pleasurable and not so pleasurable experiences. The pleasurable experiences of happiness and contentment result in feelings of settlement and balance. Instinctively we feel very much at peace with these feelings or emotions. An unpleasant experiences registers an uncomfortable feeling at a gut level, and this is stored in the subconscious. At some later time, when we are asleep, the subconscious activates the awareness that we have stored something which is causing pressure and creating an imbalance or unhappiness in us. So we role-play the situation in our sleep state using the symbology of subconscious dreaming, reliving the experience in an abstract form.

The subconscious recognises that we can't confront something in the same form it originated in because if we could have dealt with it at the time we would have. We are storing it because we couldn't deal with it, but sooner or later it has to be worked through. For example, imagine you have a problem in your work environment with a colleague. You are always feeling you are put down, with your views continually being compared unfavourably to those of the other person. Over a period of perhaps three or four months your dreams would become more active and more frequent than normal. Slowly over a period of a few months you build up more and more subconscious data about the situation. In other words, those segments of your emotions that haven't been dealt with during the day become stored over a period of time until they finally have a rather extreme effect on you. By this time you have most probably lost sight of why you're feeling the way you are. Suddenly you're feeling very depressed, you're very tired, you're very anxious and you know you've got a problem at work, but you wouldn't have a clue that it was so extreme. Yet, because you've let something get out of control over a period of time it's having a much greater effect on you than it otherwise would have.

So the dreams start to become more explicit and they extend themselves. Your subconscious actually extends its abstract form to try and get your attention. This is where we normally start to have nightmares or frightening dreams and it's the subconscious saying, 'Hey, stop ignoring me, have a look at what's bothering you.' At this time, we may pause for a stocktake of our life and really think about just what is going on, acknowledge that something is not quite right and, through the aid of the subconscious, begin to bring the problem into focus by activating a decision to resolve it. The subconscious then responds by feeding us more information to complete the solution.

Subconscious dreams can go on for years. We can structure and accumulate problems very early in our childhood and hold onto them until, as adults, we experience situations that once again trigger an awareness of the problem. We have already formed a backlog of data which can be accessed through the symbology in our subconscious dreams. That symbology can be interpreted very accurately in our adult life to plot a possible solution.

Having accumulated material on a problem for ten or fifteen years, but only at a subconscious level, you may very well not understand the root of the present problems, low self-esteem perhaps.

If you are being confronted with something you continue to ignore, there will ultimately be an eruption of a magnitude sufficient to get your attention. Your dreams become more explicit, more colourful, more exaggerated, more bizarre—perhaps even terrifying. Just as I said earlier, these explicit dreams give us tools for opening an understanding of what is going on. They open the big picture. Once we do that, we realise that the problem extends backward and not forward. We need to consciously acknowledge that we have been feeling this way for a long time. Remember that earlier I said the subconscious was crying out for attention by saying, 'Hey, stop ignoring me, have a look at what's bothering you.' Sometimes this simple conscious acknowledgment that a problem exists is enough to release the past stored data and clear out a subconscious pattern. The subconscious then registers what we resolve and works through this particular crisis to produce a positive outcome.

You may go through a period in which you have no dreams at all or, on the other side of the coin, you may find that you go through a sequence of three or four different dreams a night although you wake up feeling that you have had no dreams at all. That's very common. Many people who say they don't dream at all have disconnected from the fact that they are dreaming. Here we have a situation that has been going on for a long time; because it's been ignored, the subconscious has finally disassociated the dream role-playing from reliving the day's conscious experiences. The subconscious is still reliving the experiences, but we're not aware of them because we are disassociating from them. The result is that we don't have conscious recall of having had a dream but awaken feeling very tired because we've had a fight with ourselves in our sleep. Blocking a subconscious awareness is like trying to keep a door shut when someone is on the other side trying to pull it open. It's a very tiring experience.

On another tack, we dream not only about our problems, we dream about life in general. We dream about our aspirations, about what we want to achieve in life, about how we feel and relate to experiences, about our fears, our hopes, and all of our uncertainties. When we're lonely we dream about our wants, our desires or about being involved with someone.

Many women go through a phase in their life in which having children is an extremely important issue. If they are putting off having a child, for whatever reason, they will subconsciously begin to dream about the desire for a child, having a child, the success of a child; especially if they feel guilty or they feel they're restricting themselves from having a child, they start dreaming about their fears of having children. They may have very frightening dreams about the loss of a child.

Daydreams

Have you ever wondered why you daydream? Daydreaming is very important because it helps keep us sane. The mind needs time out from focusing on specific issues. The creative part of the mind opens when you daydream. Daydreaming is looking at situations that you would like to have in your life, watching them unfold in your mind and giving them a beginning, a middle and an end. You are actually projecting something you want and seeing it fulfilled. Daydream focusing is a very positive and powerful affirmation.

While you're daydreaming you fantasise about a whole range of things. Daydreaming is letting the mind float into a free space. It attracts all sorts of thinking. You can look at situations in romance where you would like to be with someone, fantasise about a movie star, about being your own boss or being in the position your boss is in. You see yourself in boats and planes, decked out in jewellery, you see yourself thin, and/or successful. Daydreaming is a happy time-out from everything that is going on around you.

Daydreaming can actually expand situations that are current and allow you to see or try different types of outcomes. You could see how to achieve a goal in different ways. By replaying different scenarios you get a variety of perspectives that open some very interesting possibilities in reality. You can actually change the way you do things or perhaps look at how you can approach a problem differently.

Daydreaming can also involve *déjà vu*. You may visualise or fantasise about a person you would like to meet or a situation you might like to occur. As these thoughts are unfolding you may have the distinct feeling that you actually have done this, even though you are presently only daydreaming. On the other side of that same coin is having the daydream and then later actually living the experience; it may feel very familiar although you do not remember that you created the situation in a daydream.

Daydreaming in colour means you're expanding and very creative in your awareness. You're opening up all sorts of potentials. When the daydream is in colour, it's bigger than life and it makes you feel more involved in where you are or what you're doing. It means the issue is something that you're currently working on.

Black and white daydreams represent our fears and reservations that we're not sure about what we're doing or where we're going. Having a daydream in black and white gives us the opportunity of looking at our fears and whatever our uncertainties are and resolving them.

Daydreaming can actually activate an awareness of something we didn't have an understanding of before. Because we're playing it out we can see parts of the picture in whatever the situation is that didn't make sense to us before. If it is something active in the life you're living, it can actually give you tools to work out the problem.

Daydreaming is time-out for the mind and it gives it a nice restful space. It keeps us sane, focused and functioning and it's very important to our existence. We need to be creative in our thinking, we need to express ourselves. Daydreaming is one way we actually do this. Try recording your daydreams. Keep a little book on them and then review them. You may be able to interpret them, make more sense of them, to your own surprise. (*Note:* Daydreaming is a full-on fantasy that is played out in great detail in your mind. Wishful thinking is something very short-lived, e.g. 'I wish I had a million dollars'.)

If we keep having the same daydream we may actually attract the event we are dreaming about, or something very similar to it, into our lives because we are putting a lot of focused energy into one thing. We want it, we desire it, we create it and it becomes very real for us. It may either give us the motivation to action something and make it real or attract all the necessary ingredients so it's possible.

Daydreaming can be thought of as a form of meditation because it's giving the mind a rest from activities and resolves situations we're not physically able to resolve. It allows us a space in a monotonous time frame, perhaps a very boring period in our work space, to generate new energies and become more creative in what we're doing. It can give us that extra zeal. We're then able to put extra energy into the project we're working on.

Daydreaming works very well when we're impatient. We normally wander into a space of daydreaming which stops us building up anxieties and stress. It's very functional in our everyday life.

If we have continuous daydreams about people we know, we can find they are having daydreams very similar to our own. Because we're putting a lot of energy into that focus it can actually activate another person's daydreaming state.

You may find that you're daydreaming about a particular situation coming up, perhaps a dinner party, when one of your friends rings to tell you of having had a similar daydream. That person was thinking the same thought, perhaps even at the same time you were thinking it. That's a moment of energy that's relaying and connecting with the people involved.

Some people interpret daydreaming as thinking—just another form of thinking—and to some degree that is true. We are thinking, but just as with listening to music or watching a film, it takes us away from our traditional reality and gives us a free space, physically and emotionally, that we don't normally have with our thoughts.

Daydreaming is a wonderful tool for anyone who wants to become more creative with their lives. If you utilise your daydreaming space and allow it to expand, you'll find you become a much more creative, enthusiastic, happily settled and balanced person.

Daydreaming is another way of linking with your subconscious. You are consciously thinking about your desires, your hopes, your pleasures. You are actually activating experiences that are taking place in life and extending them. It's like a war game in some ways. In your mind, you plan events and see what the outcomes would be. Then you think of what the outcome would be if you extend what is taking place into what could take place. For example: You have decided to take a typing course because your objective is to become a secretary. You begin to daydream about being successful, having a high typing speed, seeing yourself in the type of work environment you would like to be in. The reality is that you can actually bring up some of the situations that may occur if you take on that profession and you are given an opportunity to look at the result of going into that position. You begin to see the responsibilities and how time-consuming the profession is going to be if your goal is to become very successful. Then you are actually structuring an awareness that to achieve the success you desire the job will be very time consuming. So you're acknowledging that Step A (a typing course) leads to Step B (a management course or two) which will inevitably lead to Step C (executive secretary or office manager) and you may decide that this will require more effort than you wish to expend at this particular point in your life. You decide that a better short-term goal might be that of becoming a receptionist rather than a private secretary. This would allow you more time to explore your personal life. So then you begin opening other doors and exploring other possible avenues of interest. Through this daydream you've also made a statement to yourself that what you are doing is the right thing for you, or the wrong thing.

Whatever the case may be, through daydreaming we may actually make a decision which prevents concern building up and becoming a subconscious thought pattern brought up in the dream state. Thus, a daydream can actually activate a resolve for us before it gets into a deep subconscious state and needs reflection in our sleep state. Daydreaming is a productive tool which allows us to fantasise, imagine and create, to extend our imagination. Whatever we can create in an imaginary state can be facilitated in an imaginary state. So we then have an option—if we have a scenario that ends in something we don't want then we can extend the daydream into a change. This brings us to an awareness of the fact that we have perhaps taken on something with too broad a scope or perhaps more projects than we can finish. It gives us the opportunity to look at the ones that are important to us, the ones we really want to finish, as well as the ones that aren't really necessary. These need to be let go so that we can succeed with what we really want to do. It gives us an awareness of what we are capable of, what we chose to be capable of, and what we are currently choosing to do. This can eliminate a fair bit of guilt, which we always accumulate when taking on more than we can handle.

Once a project is begun, we feel obligated to finish it. However, as soon as we realise that we've bitten off too much, we can get confused about what we are doing, we get into that awful cycle of being tired, anxious and uncertain. If we don't daydream and don't extend ourselves then we might drop everything we're doing, let it all go and try to start again. That's the wrong way to attack the problem. This way actually stops us from realising we have actually taken on too much. Within a very short period of time we again attack something in the very same way, once again taking on more than we can handle. The effect can be disastrous. We get into the same position again, eventually feeling as if we have too much on our plate and letting go of it all.

Using daydreaming as a tool can help us realise that something has to go before we can fulfil ourselves and achieve balance. Once we work this reality out, we're able to access it more and more. This gives us the opportunity to become aware of what we are able to take on. Some people, of course, can extend themselves more than others so that taking on multiple projects is not a problem.

If we are working through problems at a pace we can handle mentally, emotionally and physically they will not overwhelm us. Let's say we are deciding to landscape our garden and at the same time rebuild our house. The two projects are interfering with each other in terms of time and cost. We start getting concerned about which is the greater priority and we lose sight of the original goal. Through daydreaming we can see the potential of letting one go for a while, finishing one project and then the other. In other words we realise that a time frame is very important. We cannot do everything within a given boundary of time. Not all situations can occur in the same boundary of time and have to be extended.

This life is filled with extenuating circumstances. Our free will and choice allows us to take on anything we choose. Our daydreaming makes us realise how much we have taken on and the effect of it. We can still continually extend ourselves into what we want in our lives without it overwhelming us and without it putting us in a position we cannot handle. Subconscious dreaming allows us to attack our fears and resolve our life crises. It allows us access to our own power, our own potential, and to direct ourselves in life. It gives us a certain amount of fulfilment in life and allows us to feel or give ourselves a sense of strength and balance. That is why both kinds of dreaming are so important.

Everyone dreams, but at times we choose not to recall our dreams. Sometimes they are so intricate and involved, so loaded with symbolism, that we lose sight of what they are. The more confusing a dream is, the more confusing our life is. Normally a confusing dream means denial, that we are denying something very obvious which is having an extreme effect on us. Symbolism reproduces that confusion in a way that can give you access to the problem from a different angle. If you use your dreams as a tool you will find that you fulfil much more in your physical existence.

Take notice of the warnings that you get in dreams. It isn't the abstract which is important here but the fact that your subconscious is trying to get through to you that you are having a real life problem which you aren't coming to grips with that needs to be worked through. Your subconscious isn't intentionally trying to frighten you into believing that the abstract is the reality. It's trying to make you aware that you are creating something as an abstract which you are denying as a reality. Because you are not doing anything with it, your subconscious has a need to show you, perhaps in a somewhat frightening manner, that it's time you woke up to look at what's happening when you are awake. Recording your dreams, even if only in part, will help you to eventually see a pattern that will bring about the conscious awareness necessary to initiate some kind of resolution. You should look at the symbolism in your dreams in your own way, because symbolism is a very personal thing. Although there are some general meanings for particular symbols, there are many more which will have meaning to you alone.

First list the symbols in your dreams and then ask yourself what they mean to you. Then make a list of all the things that a symbol represents. Start a little book of your own, listing your personal symbolism. You will be surprised at what you uncover and how you actually start to understand your own dreams through doing this.

Make your list of symbols without thinking about the kind of dream they appeared in. What does a flower mean to you? Different colours, different types of flowers, faces, animals, structures, houses, offices, roads, cars, water, weather—list anything else you can think of. Then slowly take a mental stroll through your daily experiences with all of these things and see what they feel like, what they actually mean at the time.

For example, what does it feel like to be in a park? Is it a comfortable experience for you? When is it not a comfortable experience, and why is it not? Write down the positive and negative qualities. Surprise, you've collated a book on symbolism that you can relate to at a later date. Now after dreaming you can retrieve the symbols and go through your book to see what is appropriate. This way you give yourself an understanding of what you're going through and what your experience really means.

Nightmares

Another type of subconscious dream is the nightmare. When we go to sleep at night with worries, concerns, confusion or uncertainty travelling through our mind, we open the potential of extending our dream state into a nightmare. A nightmare is just another way for our subconscious to express a difficulty that we are having in our awakened state, but in a rather extreme way. Again the subconscious is merely giving us a nudge to look at a problem or an issue so that it will not have such a detrimental effect on us. This is why we normally remember the dreams which are bizarre or nightmarish. These dreams stay so fresh and vivid in our minds that we usually walk around consciously trying to work out what was going on during the night!

Nightmares, however, can be very abstract and difficult to interpret. A sequence of continuous dreams or nightmares can become more complex as time passes. Normally the subconscious puts us through a lot of feelings and emotions with a nightmare, trying to get us to release all our fears and uncertainties so that we are not storing them and bottling them up.

How can we overcome nightmares?

There are several easy processes that we can use to assist us in getting to know and understand the underlying cause or issue, in becoming more aware and in touch with what the nightmares are trying to express to our conscious state, and to help us actually eliminate the nightmares, releasing them so they don't reoccur.

Firstly, on awakening from a nightmare it is important that you record exactly what the basis of the nightmare was.

Secondly, you need to record what your awakened feeling was. Were you breathless, did you find it difficult to make your eyes focus, was your perception unclear, were your senses disorientated? Take a mental note of your physical condition at the point of awakening and exactly how you felt: disrupted, angry, upset, depressed, frightened, emotional.

Basically, at the point of awakening your main concern has to be clearing up and rebalancing your perspective. Take a deep breath, relax and release whatever it is you've experienced and note it on paper. Mentally acknowledge to yourself, 'I am releasing and clearing this issue. I am letting it go and I am going to deal with it and look at it in its proper form.'

Now, if you have the opportunity of looking at the nightmare at that point, well and good. If not, prepare yourself for the day but at the end of the day set aside some time where you can actually sit down and look in detail at what you've written.

Firstly, look at the emotions and feelings that came up for you that morning and ask yourself how that would relate to the symbolism or situation you recorded. See if you can find a common denominator.

Example: You awoke feeling very frightened with the symbol of seeing yourself falling and unable to get up. The interpretation is that you are feeling out of control with a situation in your life.

Example: You have awakened feeling out of touch with your feelings, with the memory of seeing someone that you care about leaving or going away. The reality of this is that you are not communicating well with someone and you are frightened of losing them or having a rift or separation. In this case you need to communicate on a more open level with the person and work with your feelings.

Example: You were sitting on a boat, seeing sharks swarming all around you, threatening to bite and perhaps even succceeding in attacking you. The feelings are of extreme tiredness and confusion. The interpretation of this is that you are feeling very drained. People are taking a lot out of you and expecting a lot from you while you have given beyond your level of capacity for survival and are tired and exhausted. Your subconscious is literally telling you to stop giving so much of yourself out.

Example: You were walking along, and talking to someone whose face you don't identify, with snakes or serpents snapping at your feet. The feelings are of insecurity and of being a little lost and disconnected from other people. The reality of this is normally the fear of someone talking behind your back, of others discussing things about you.

Case history

First night: *I had a farm of strawberries and the family and I were trying to sell them from the side of a busy road. I could see the back of my son while he was selling strawberries; then the road got very muddy and we weren't selling any more strawberries. Then the scene changed—I was with people who were throwing rubbish at each other. It was like a neighbourhood brawl.*

Second night: *I was inside a house when three dark men came to the front door. I was quite alarmed by their appearance and feared they would harm me, so I hurriedly locked the security door. They glared at me and I knew they would harm me although they tried to reassure me they would not.*

This led to another dream or two not remembered, but on the third night I remember being in a crowd of people in a theatre foyer. I went up to a group of people I knew to ask if there was a booking office upstairs. I felt I had to meet someone up there.

Fourth night: *I was terrified of someone walking into the bedroom where I was sleeping. I felt as if I was being choked, it seemed so real. Lots of grey colour. I was terrified.*

Fifth night: *I dreamed of my brother who had recently had his leg amputated and saw him in hospital having more work done on him. We were with his wife. There were tickets everywhere, but as I looked at them more closely they were only stubs.*

This sequence of continuous dreaming was a nightmare reoccurring for this man. The message is very clear: he was dealing with his own feelings of inadequacy relating to his brother's amputation. The first night was the reliving of a normal family activity that turned into an unpleasant event, his own fears showing toward the changes in his own life and his brother's. The second night the terror of the dark men represents his own inner feelings of insecurity and fear of upcoming changes in his own life as well as dealing once again with his brother, whom I feel is a common thread throughout each night's dreaming along with the man himself looking at the changes in his own life. On the third night the feeling of being on show is significant, with the dreamer feeling as if everyone is looking to him for an answer or direction. On the fourth night suffocation represents his own inner fears mounting, and the final night is the reality that changes have already taken place in his life. The stubs represent the event having taken place. Whole tickets would have been an event about to take place.

Separately these dreams appear to be very confusing. They would most likely have been easily forgotten if they were not recorded. Together, the pattern is quite unmistakeable and the total message is fairly easy to work out.

Once you have looked at the feelings and all the memories that you've had of the nightmare experience you can normally give it some form of understanding. It tells you if you have pressures going on in your job or if something is occurring where you feel out of control. Once you are aware of your dream and nightmare state letting you know that this is the case, that you're feeling out of control and helpless, you will be able to take control again.

The first thing to do is mentally affirm to yourself, 'I acknowledge what this nightmare is about. It makes sense to me and I am now going to do something about it.' By verbalising this you are telling your subconscious to let go of the need to repeat the nightmare in subsequent sleep states. Mentally affirm and ask that you be given or shown a way of resolving the problem, and this is exactly what will happen with your next dream state. You will find that you move forward into seeing an achievement level or a change which will give you some perspective on how to approach the situation more clearly.

Once we see things more clearly we are able to action some change in our physical life, which in turn changes the make-up of our dreaming and the extremes of what we feel in our sleep state. A normal sleep pattern then returns, along with a normal dreaming pattern.

Past-life recall

The second type of dream state is the past-life recall. Here we experience a very graphic dream with bright vivid colours. We feel as though we are in the dream, yet different somehow, and on awakening have an intense feeling of *déjà vu*. 'It felt too real to be just a dream,' is a frequent comment.

The past-life recall dream occurs when we are moving into an understanding in our present life or are about to go through some change in our awareness. Accessing data from a past life is necessary to help us with our experience in the present. This type of dreaming also occurs when we meet people we have known before or visit places we have been to before. It will also occur if we move into a career or open up potential talents that we have had in other lifetimes.

Past-life recall dreams normally project in our minds as expansive, bright, vivid dreams which feel out of context with life. The scenery may look very old, even ancient. You may feel as if you are in the eighteenth century, in the middle of a movie you have seen on television. In all likelihood you are accessing your own past, exploring where you have been and what you have experienced at a time that is very appropriate to you. Once again, this kind of dream may seem out of context and very difficult to interpret. However, it's less complicated and much easier to understand than a subconscious dream because situations are in a normal form. In other words, the scenery is not abstract; even though it may not be a type of scenery you relate to now it's not out of context with your mind. You can actually understand what the situation represents.

If you see yourself happy as you dream, you're accessing a pleasurable experience of the past. When it's a little disorientating and upsetting then you're accessing something that was not so pleasant.

Past-life recall comes up for many reasons. We need to access past data to assist us with where we are now, when we are experiencing something that we have experienced before. Accessing past-life data lets us use it as a tool to help us work through our present experience and make the most of it.

Past-life recall can be a *déjà vu* experience because we have indeed experienced it before. It is something we have actually done so it won't feel unfamiliar to us, just slightly out of reach. Sometimes the past-life recall stage eludes us, and we're not quite sure what we are tapping into. Our memory is only bringing up a portion, a very minor portion, of an experience. Once again we have tools we can use to assist us. By asking the mind to expand and allow us more access in our wakened state to past-life recall, over a period of time we will allow ourselves access to it. Daily affirmations just prior to sleep accomplish this nicely, e.g. 'I now choose to awaken past-life memory beneficial to me in this life.'

We may have past-life recall when we need people we've had previous experiences with. They may be people we have actually met in this lifetime whom we have forgotten about. We can reactivate a memory of that meeting through this type of dream state. We can then compare the experience of the past life with our present needs. If the person was a very close friend in a past lifetime then the potential for a friendship in this lifetime is also there. Past-life recall can be confusing because we can actually bring forth more than one lifetime in our dream and thus be accessing lots of collective thought. If we record the dream we can evaluate it in the light of the present life situation. We can see a pattern developing from pieces gathered during several lifetimes. Once again we affirm that we wish to look at all these lifetimes but we'd like them expanded and to appear one by one.

We also access past-life recall when we're expanding our own sensitivity, getting more in touch with ourselves. We may open an awareness of where we were before and what we have achieved before which gives us insight into the future direction of our life. It can open up our self-confidence and enhance our abilities. This increases our current achievement potential and expands our level of creativity.

Dreams on past-life recall

Once you are out of body, time no longer exists. You can go forward, you can stay in the present or you can go back into the past. If you are dealing with something important in your life you may trigger deep cellular memories stored within your chakra centres and bring up information or data which is relevant from a past-life experience. While in an out-of-body state you can actually step back into a past life and re-live the experience.

You do this to bring understanding and clarity of that life experience forward to help with the situation you are currently in. You can tap into skills and structures from the past to help you understand why you feel a particular way now, or you can project potential into the future with an understanding of what you have been in the past.

If you have awakened a memory of a past-life experience, re-experienced it and brought it forward to the present, it can trigger an awakening within your deep subconscious of something you are storing now that you have not resolved. This can cause very abstract dreaming, taking you into an extreme mode of symbolism and perhaps even to a nightmare. An emotion or a situation that you secretly do not wish to resolve can cause trauma, resulting in a nightmare.

Out-of-body experiences

The third type of dream is the out-of-body experience, or external flight syndrome. This can happen when we have a need to be free of our physical body and astrally project. Our etheric body leaves the physical body to have a rest and travels into the future, past or present on one of the seven levels of the astral plane. We can see people, places or situations and events that take place in our past, present or future. A typical example is dreaming that a friend has taken you to dinner. A few days later this situation occurs, in the same restaurant where the same food is served. Another example is seeing someone in a dream you have not seen for a long time and meeting them not long afterwards. We can see an event being cancelled due to the weather or a friend telling us she is moving into a new house—you know in advance what type of house she will move into. We also call this precognition, which is seeing an event or situation before it happens.

Everybody has out-of-body experiences. When you go to sleep at night and your body is resting, your soul or spirit steps out of your physical body and goes travelling. You're getting out basically to stretch your legs and have some space from your physical body. Your soul or spirit goes on a journey through the astral or projects into the future and has a look at upcoming events.

From time to time everybody does a bit of astral travelling. When you have completed a period of review and storage of data from your awakened state, the mind goes into a different space. It opens to your dream state and it also allows you 'time out' from your body.

You also astrally project when you need time out from mental or emotional experiences. You go out-of-body to one of the seven levels of the astral plane. What is an out-of-body experience? As the essence of your being (your soul) leaves the sleeping human body it journeys into a dimension which is void of time and space. You may meet people you know for purely social purposes or to resolve problems. You may also meet people you will encounter at a later time in the conscious, physical world. It allows your consciousness to expand beyond its physical form and to re-enter the body refreshed. In this space we integrate ideas and concepts which we then bring to manifestation in our awakened state.

When we return to our bodies we can sometimes feel frozen or paralysed; sometimes we cannot even speak. The sensation passes very quickly as we come awake. This occurs because we are re-entering our physical body and have not quite properly aligned the soul with the physical body.

Inhibitory neural mechanisms occurring during REM (rapid eye movement) sleep cause the body to experience *atonia*, a loss of muscle tone, resulting in a state of semi-paralysis. It becomes almost impossible for the dreaming REM sleeper to move. I believe this occurs because the soul or essence of life has left the physical body to journey into the astral, a belief which does not preclude the following theory: Some researchers believe that this change to semi-paralysis may take place to protect sleepers from physically responding to or acting out their dreams. Sleeptalking and sleepwalking, in fact, have been found to occur during NREM (non-rapid eye movement) sleep, when the body is better able to move.[5]

External flight syndrome

The dimensions we call time doesn't exist once we're out of our body. Time exists only in the physical realm. We can actually step out of our body into the astral and visit a particular person. Later on we see the friends that we visited during the night and they say, 'I felt you were in the room with me last night',

---

[5]John P. Dworetzky, *Psychology*, 2nd ed., West Publishing Co., St Paul, Minnesota

or 'I had a dream about you last night'. They normally have recall of the event or the situation just as we do.

Out-of-body experience is a natural phenomenon—it's something we all do. There is nothing to be frightened of because we are in total control of what we're doing, and we never lose our body. The body is merely resting and recovering from its daily activities. We're getting out basically to stretch our legs and have some space from it.

Occasionally when we return to our bodies in a hurry, for example, if we've been woken suddenly by someone or the phone has rung and we've been jarred awake, we can feel very disorientated because we haven't aligned properly back into our bodies. The technique that I recommend for realignment of your spirit with your physical body is to focus from the tips of your toes all the way up to the top of your head. You will feel much more in focus and aligned with yourself. Another way of doing it is just to stroke your nose gently.

If you leave yourself in this disoriented state you end up with a headache. The pressure is caused by not aligning properly—it's like having an equilibrium balance problem or an inner ear infection. You are just a little out of focus and that can be very disorienting.

Our out-of-body experiences can occasionally be very traumatic; we can come back and in our awakened state feel as if we've been through some sort of a trauma. This happens because we have projected into the future and had a look at circumstances or situations around people we are concerned about. We may see friends fighting, for example. We come back with the memory of the argument which normally is triggered at the time of the argument. We think, 'Well, this feels really familiar. I feel as if I've experienced this before.'

We can look at happy events too. We can see friends having babies and feel overwhelmed, having prior memory of the baby's sex, of the delivery, of the experience of the mother.

Out-of-body experiences allow us to catch up with people we don't get to see very often—relatives or friends travelling overseas or who live a long distance from us. When we have been travelling to see loved ones or friends, it's quite common for them to telephone or write to explain that they felt the same way, that there was a need to ring up and say, 'Hi.' They felt aware of your presence at a particular time on a particular day or generally over a time period.

There are people who through higher forms of meditation can open up an awareness and a total recall of out-of-body experiences and actually meet people who are able to do the same type of meditation and focus. Although I can't quote the exact source, I remember reading a few years ago about a series of studies regarding astral travel (out-of-body experiences) which were conducted in America. A group of individuals of varying degrees of awareness and meditative abilities were paired together and told to plan a meeting at a given location (I recall one of the locations as a bus which was en route between two neighbouring towns) during their sleep state. The individuals adjourned to their separate abodes and returned the following day. Each person was able to accurately recount details of the location as well as the conversation.

For the majority, out-of-body experiences are not something we usually recall. Sometimes we have memories of stepping into the future, so that when it becomes the present we feel familiar with it. This is a *déjà vu* structure as well because we are actually going into an experience that we've glimpsed or viewed prior to the experience.

Out-of-body experience allows us freedom from our physical body. It is a wonderful space of free time, time-out from being limited inside the structure of the physical body. It is a time when our body is at rest and our spirit has freedom to move. When our physical body is preparing to awaken our spirit realigns with it and we awaken gently, normally and slowly. This is a natural process and totally automatic.

Sometimes, though, we can be jarred awake by a noise or disruption before our spirit has aligned properly with our physical body, as mentioned earlier, and feel out of synchronisation with ourselves all day. This is because we have jumped back into our bodies too quickly. If this process takes place very quickly it can bring on a state of shock which may cause us to see a lot of things in our bedroom that frighten us a little or cause concerns. We may even see colourful spots of energy through the room.

Normally our guides or loved ones say goodbye and watch us go back into our bodies. It is they who appear as spots of energy. It is a very loving, caring space of time that they have shared with us and their presence is their way of saying they care about us. They just watch us go back into alignment with our body and say goodnight to us or good morning. There isn't anything to be frightened of. We are very protected when we are out of body. If we relax at this point and just focus on our physical body, from the tips of our toes to the top of our head, we can realign properly and awake properly feeling refreshed.

CHAPTER 3

Symbolism and its Meaning

Remember that we talked briefly about data processing and its various levels at the beginning of Chapter 1. Here I intend to expand that information.

There are four levels of data processing in the mind. The first level involves the collection of data. We do this through our five senses: seeing, touching, tasting, hearing and smelling. Everything in the environment that is capable of transmitting data to us through one of these five senses does so, whether we are conscious of it or not. By that I mean you may be looking at a rose bush across the yard while smelling a frangipani located at half of that distance as a car drives by. Your conscious mind is on the rose bush but also registered in your subconscious is the smell of the frangipani and the sight and sound of the car.

The second level involves filing the data. This is just temporarily putting away all of the data not currently in use for later processing as necessary. You may be looking at the rose bush, considering putting one in your own yard, and taking no notice of the car until it runs into another car parked on the side of the road. Your attention is now focused on the car accident and whether anyone was hurt or the extent of damage done. Your mind puts away the sight of the rose and the scent of the frangipani and the previous position of the car up to the point of the accident. It then turns your undivided attention to the car.

The third level is where you review your files to determine whether any of them require further processing or if they can go to deep storage (the archive). Your subconscious places the various files in a queue in the order of their importance. The trauma of the car accident would go to the front of the line, followed by the rose bush, while the frangipani would go into deep or permanent storage as there is no action required. Any traumas not resolved by this review are brought up and re-evaluated continually for a short period. The subconscious eventually recognises that you are not willing or perhaps able to clear out the traumatic data in its original form so it gives you another opportunity to do so by creating the same format in symbolism. The subconscious's objective is for the symbolism to trigger an awakening memory which alerts you to the fact that you are still storing unresolved traumas.

If you look at the symbolism of your dreams you can reactivate the file and open it up to its true form. In the dream state you can show yourself the actual event so you can resolve or release it.

Normally by the time you allow your memory to store at the third level the problem is not something you understand in a conscious form. Your symbols are very abstract, you do not understand what they mean and so the trauma becomes very difficult to work with. Through this book you are going to learn to open up and connect back to a memory, understanding your symbolism through the keys in the section 'Self-Help Techniques and Alternatives—Meditation' (page 90).

If you do not work through a problem, over a period of time the subconscious allocates all the data belonging to it down to the fourth level, or archives, where you have a filing system that is inactive—that is, the archives do not respond to the triggering mechanism of experiences in your sleep state, but have gone into a dormant state.

This is the level that you have to extend, either through deep hypnosis or actioning with symbolism and keys, to open up and bring the trauma back up to a higher level to resolve and work through.

You actually have a facility within your subconscious for clearing and releasing locked emotions. Think of a storage cupboard full of objects, some useful and some useless. Just like cleaning out this old cupboard, you are continually dream-releasing a lot of data or experiences that don't need to be allocated or filed because you have resolved and worked through a situation. Your mind is just acknowledging that process through your dreams. You also have a memory pool where every life experience is stored. All your dreams and all the informational data that you collect through your life experience are recorded as this level, the fohatic pool (see page 23).

The fohatic pool of consciousness in the physical form is stored in the human aura. Depending on the magnitude of the trauma, your refusal to deal with it or resolve it in the conscious state can actually create a physical illness or horrific nightmares. This inevitably occurs when you just refuse to resolve something in your life.

A reminder note to your conscious about something unresolved is sometimes called a 'Freudian slip'. This happens when something just 'pops out' because memory (mind retrieval of an unresolved file) is triggered by the event currently in front of you. This is the point where you could still do something about resolving the memory before it goes into the deepest level of storage.

The brain functions much like a central processing unit (CPU) in a computer. It relays data to and from storage, makes decisions regarding data, does calculations with numbers and data information and generally serves as a relay station and as short term storage for recently relevant data, much like the Random Access Memory (RAM) of a computer, by running the current life program and on-screen data before it is sent to permanent storage. Being much more efficient than a computer, the brain can receive data gathered by any of the five senses (sight, hearing, smell, taste and touch) and send it directly to long-term storage without any processing, even though it may not be relevant at the moment. For example: While you are talking to someone, out the corner of your eye you see two people having an argument, although you can't hear what is being said. It doesn't involve you at the moment and as it has no immediate impact on your immediate situation you dismiss it as inconsequential. The next day one of those people isn't speaking to you and you don't know why. Weeks go by and still the person isn't talking to you. Even though that person isn't important to you, you begin to wonder about their strange behaviour. Finally you have a dream about being a wealthy prince who's fallen in love with a princess from another land. The problem is, she won't have anything to do with you. Ultimately you discover someone has falsely told her you have a disease and won't live long. When she learns the truth she returns your love, you marry and live happily ever after. When you awaken and go to work the next day you confront the person who isn't speaking to you and find out he was told some untruth about you when he had the original argument we spoke of earlier. When you sort it all out, the person gets back on side, your relationship gets back to normal and may even be stronger than it was before.

What has happened here is that your eyes picked up relevant information and sent it directly to your subconscious for storage. It was given back to you in a dream to show you a solution. Had you ignored the dream and continued to worry about the problem it would have come up again in a different dream and become progressively more bizarre until it became a nightmare.

Another function of the brain is to work with current programming of the physical body. The most common example of this is psychosomatic illness. Dr

Maxwell Maltz is well known for the book *Psycho-Cybernetics* in which he details the ease with which the human mind can be programmed to make the physical body ill. Another book relevant to this area is John Harrison's *Love Your Disease*.

We are just coming into an age where we are hearing more and more cases of people with incurable diseases who have miraculously cured themselves through 'creative visualisation'. They believe they are well and the body responds in kind.

Types of symbolism

Primitive-state symbols, another name for the symbols you see in dreams, reveal an inability to decipher your situation. You don't have enough knowledge or understanding to sort out the meaning of your dreams. Therefore, your subconscious feeds your dreams with symbols which are in some way representative of the situation but allow you to see it from a different angle and may give you some insight into the resolution.

The symbols represent the structures you know in life such as houses, cups, things that you could relate to your home life or work structure. They may also represent feelings, emotions, striving influences, health status, how you feel and relate to your emotions, physical or sensual experiences at birth and death.

The family structure can represent not only the problems or situations that you're dealing with in your family life, but how you deal with people generally or how you construct your friendships and work relationships.

Symbols that are unknown to us come from a higher consciousness. They can be symbolic of a precognitive state, in other words, an awareness of a situation coming up or an answer to a problem (our own or someone else's) before we know what that problem is. (Precognitive—having the knowledge before the situation arises.)

Through a higher consciousness we can be viewing our own future at a higher ego level, foretelling our own direction, having perception about where we could be going in life. Linking up with our friends and relatives and seeing them in a position of success or in a very fruitful outcome is symbolic of this level of dreaming. We may see totally abstract symbols we are unable to understand which our mind does not recover or remember in the wakened state. This is symbolic of situations to come which we don't yet understand. We are preparing for change, to accept new data in our awareness and understanding. Things with spirit forms are normally representative of the way we perceive life and death. Our spiritual perception is opening to a higher self perhaps, pervading our dream state to communicate with us.

Symbolism pulls down the walls of any structures that we formulate in our understanding of thought. Thought has no time barrier. We can pick up past experiences in this life as well as experiences in past lives through our dream states. One may come into total contact with a consciousness or an understanding of what God is. We can unravel our own prophetic awareness of what our spirituality is through our dream state.

You can exist in the astral levels of the dream state for a very long period because you are still very earthbound. The physical body regenerates and rests but the mind is active throughout your sleep state. The only times it frees itself are when you go into an out-of-body experience, or when you meditate. These are the two states that work with total release, where the mind has time out, and they are both very necessary for life. If you don't meditate, your system will react to the need for astral projection. You might find if you do meditate quite a lot that you have more recall with astral projection than people who don't meditate. People who meditate are much more in touch with their spirit essence and they can feel the separation.

Many people are frightened of the concept of astral projection until they experience it and realise that they are in complete control and can come back at will. What is this weird sensation that people talk about? It can be quite a scary thought, but doing it is no more frightening than going to sleep at night. Nothing will harm you. You have natural abilities and your body responds to those natural abilities. There is a need for spiritual separation during sleep. You may sit in your lounge room and just feel the room you live in. You may go and visit a loved one. You may go higher and have an astral projection to another plane of existence, of which you have no recall at all, and that's very, very normal. Few people have recall of their astral projection through the sleep state. It's much more likely to happen through focus with meditation and the conscious awareness that they're leaving their body and going through the processes. I would guess that 99 per cent of the population at one point in their life have had an out-of-body experience that they can recall, whether they relate to the status of an astral projection or not.

Dream symbols

A lot of the dreams we have are symbolic. When the dream is very accurate and fits into a situation that you can make sense of, it normally means it's a current situation in your life and you're extending it in your dream state.

The majority of things that you view through life are stored and collected in the mind and may have an effect on you over a long period of time. Your subconscious makes you aware of anything that you are storing and its effect on you, projecting the understanding of your collection of feelings, thoughts and ideas in a symbolic format. When you're asleep you frequently see things which actually represent something else in your life. We may see ourselves falling into a very deep gully or into a river. Falling dreams mean that we're feeling as if we're out of control in some situation. We're not on top of it. Something is getting on top of us. We feel helpless and uncertain.

Prehistoric symbols such as rocks, dragons and prehistoric animals, being stuck in a jungle, in a desert, or in an extreme structure of weather such as a cyclone or a hurricane leave you feeling as if you are incapable of achieving or that you do not have the abilities that you need in a particular situation to be successful. You fear failure and believe that failure is innately yours.

Animals like rabbits, kittens or puppies, baby chicks or deer represent your vulnerability. You may be feeling very open and vulnerable or very content, happy and in balance with your inner child. If you see the animals playing, it means that you are feeling joyous and happy.

Many symbols have more than one meaning and sometimes those several meanings do not appear compatible. The correct interpretation can easily be found when you look at the symbol in the context of the entire dream or even of a series of dreams the same night or over an extended period. This is also why it is good to go through the process of determining what your own symbols mean to you.

Index of symbolism

Fears and anxieties are always represented as unpleasant experiences in a dream. Happiness is always something beautiful and overwhelming.

Abdomen Seeing an abundant feminine figure is significant of prosperity or financial gain. An injury to the stomach or bruising is significant of feeling hurt by someone that you care about, being distressed about something someone said to you. Strange markings on the stomach area are relevant to trying to release anger or frustration, or of getting in touch with your own emotions and having them overwhelm you.

Abortion Aborting a child signifies purging yourself of some emotional feeling, or totally blocking out a sensation that you are feeling or experiencing, being out of focus, not looking at something correctly.

Abundance Fostering growth in your creativity, the way you are perceiving things, the gifts that you accept and work towards.

Accidents Generally car, pedestrian, ship and most other accidents relate to a fear of becoming undone in something that you're doing at the present time, including relationships. It signifies that the relationship isn't going to be all that you expect it to be.

Acorns Significant when one is trying to accumulate finance for a particular goal. It is the subconscious telling you that you are starting to file and store all that is necessary for you at the present time.

Acting/Performances You are not able to express your emotions and feelings directly to a person. The situation in the play is somehow relevant to your current life.

Alien Outer space character. Symbolic of something out of your reach or your understanding. Difficulty understanding how others can see you or relate to you in the way they do. Your perception being out of focus.

Alligator Symbolic of the jaws of justice. Normally letting us know we have done something wrong that we can't admit to ourselves or others.

Angel Very relevant to your guide trying to communicate with you while you are asleep.

Animals   Generally significant of how we are feeling, our vulnerability, what we are trying to camouflage in ourselves. If it is an angry animal, we are camouflaging our anger. If it is a happy, carefree animal, we are trying to feel footloose and fancy free. If it is a cat (can be any animal, sometimes your personal totem, but most frequently a cat), sitting on or next to something familiar to you, then it is not the animal but the item it is sitting on that your attention is being drawn to.

Animals flying   Seeing animals flying or seeing yourself flying represents freedom. You feel as though you have just released a burden and broken free of your restrictions, self-imposed or otherwise. You have moved into something that gives you great freedom and scope. Normally the ability is within yourself to give yourself permission to have that freedom and scope.

Ants   Ants or very small creatures featuring in a dream are a representation of being fastidious, needing to be very fussy about the most minute detail. A large swarm of bees or ants represents a large fear of small details.

Antiques   Significant with a feeling of being out of synchronisation with yourself and the rest of the world. You are not in the place where you should be at a particular time, or not keeping up with current information.

Army   An army marching signifies the gaining of strength and defending yourself physically or verbally.

Armour   Suits of armour definitely represent a need for protection. You feel encumbered because you are exposing your vulnerability and the armour is not thick enough. You are looking for more protection, usually during some emotional crisis.

Artist   Seeing yourself painting or drawing is reflective of your desire to express your ideas and creativity.

Babies   A baby being born, even if it is a traumatic experience, represents growth and an amplification of your own self-expansion. It also means that you are nurturing yourself to be whole, whole in the sense of being both vulnerable and strong, being in control of your own vulnerability and strength. A baby can also represent a primitive state, or stepping into the future and witnessing some growth or expansion for yourself or for someone close to you. Prominent or positive changes may be coming up for you.

Ballet/Ballerina   Going into a self-approval period where you are starting to accept the creative side of your own personality or that of someone close to you.

Being exposed   Being exposed where others can see you in a communal/public shower or toilet represents that your feelings are being hurt by others and you are accepting that without being confrontational. It also represents your inner vulnerability and feeling vulnerable to yourself or to others.

Birth   The stimulation of new awareness and understanding, accepting some deep part of your own understanding as being very legitimate in life. The beginning of something new for you.

Blender   Stirring up trouble for others, or others stirring up trouble for you.

Camera   Someone taking a picture of you reflects feeling that you are on show. You taking pictures of others signifies trying to store memory and having difficulty absorbing data or information. A camera could also be significant of the emotional space that you're in, hanging onto the present and not going forward into the future.

Candy   Striped—significant of a body disorder. For a female, possibly hormonal, for a man, immune deficiency.

Cardiac arrest   Going through a great deal of pain or pressure. Too many debts, feeling weighed down with responsibility or fears and anxieties. This is a subconscious warning that you should take better care of your health—your worries are having an effect on you.

Cats   Black cats jumping on you in a dream indicate that you're not looking at something, not resolving an issue or taking notice of something that is affecting you while wallowing in it. Cats moving around you or in your environment generally mean an awakening of your own spiritual growth, your sensitivity, that you're coming into a focus of knowledge and understanding. To see a cat and be very frightened of it means that you're frightened of what you're seeing in yourself. Seeing a cat in a fight represents a tug-of-war that you're having with yourself, an imbalance in your decision making. (*also see* Animals)

Children   Small and well behaved children could be for a woman the opening up of maternal or children's problems or issues of children in life. The dream children giving someone a hard time represents difficulties you are having with the child within yourself or with children directly.

Cigarette   Seeing yourself smoking may be relevant to the fact that you have just given up and you have a strong problem with it. It can also be very much connected with anxiety.

Clocks   Clocks going off, alarms ringing, signify that our subconscious is trying to tell us to wake up to something we are not looking at.

Clothes   Clothes that are too small signify something that you feel you have outgrown, an expression or an attitude or some sort of materialistic structure. Clothes that are too big signify struggling with a promotion, with study or a new idea, trying to grow into a new space.

Clovers (four-leafed)   Always significant of clarity and awareness. Sometimes of growth, with money and prosperity.

Cobwebs   Very significant of wealth and prosperity. A change in attitude and circumstances.

Coin   A coin lost reflects disbelief in oneself, lack of confidence, imbalance. A coin found reflects recovery of self-esteem and confidence.

Curtains   Curtains blowing in the wind represent integration of inner harmony and balance, higher spiritual harmony, opening the curtains to understanding, or an inner belief exposed and opened.

Darkness   Being out of touch with something that is bothering you. Not being able to work out what is disturbing you about a person or situation. Something that represents any unknown quantity.

Dark and light   Dark gloomy dreams represent our fears and reservations. Bright sunny ones represent our creative expansion and potential; they can also mean that we're more in control than we realise of the circumstances that we're dreaming about.

Death   Normally the release of something and accepting growth and change, the change within the self. The ending of a situation. Like the Death Card in a Tarot deck, death or seeing someone dying doesn't represent the death of a person but means that *change* has or is about to take place, that you've actually lost part of yourself or that you're seeing someone else lose a part of themselves.

It's quite common for parents, as their children grow up, to have dreams of death. It's the parent letting the child go to become an adult. This usually occurs when the parent has reservations about projecting the relationship structure as an adult to an adult, which is totally different from the relationship of an adult to a child. The subconscious is merely dealing with that situation as a death scene.

Disease   Seeing your body covered in splotches or going through some fever is related to the body taking on some form of self-punishment, seeing something of yourself that offends you or being deeply hurt and offended by someone or something. Sometimes a procognitive warning to pay more attention to your health.

Distress   Whether you're feeling an emotion, distress, upset or people are not there to support you in a dream, is significant of you losing your confidence base. Basically you lack confidence about yourself at that particular time.

Doctor/Physician   The need to be healed and looked after or acknowledging that one should see a doctor about something disturbing you. Perhaps a friend needs to see or be attended by a physician.

Doors   Lots and lots of doors opening up mean that you have accepted a change in your life. You're motivating that change. Doors that are closed, that you can't open or access, mean you feel left out of a situation where others are involved and you can't participate—but closed doors normally symbolise the fact that you're not letting yourself in, you're choosing to be outside because of your own belief that you are unable to participate, not somebody else's belief.

Dropping/Breaking   Dropping or breaking a bottle of liquid symbolises an argument about to happen, which you are going to start.

Elevator   Going up is significant of travel and change. Going down means that you have been disappointed.

Elves/Fairies   The inner child being explored and developed. Opening up to the inner child within oneself. Happiness and success.

Empty house   An empty house or a strange environment symbolises that something has changed in your awareness. You've seen something in a different way and you don't know how to handle it or deal with it. You're going through a soul-searching period in your life. You're looking for answers, you're trying to uncover the depth of your own awareness.

Faith   Extreme faith in a dream is significant of internal will-power and strength.

Falling   Being out of control, whether in your life situation or a particular circumstance. The sensation of falling, just as you drop off to sleep represents the transition into an out-of-body experience.

Falsehood   Finding out that something is wrong or that someone has deceived you. An awareness of lies or deceit. The subconscious is being prodded to awaken and recognise what is happening in the everyday awakened state.

Family   Dreaming of different members of the family normally means that you are resolving an issue with them during your sleep-state that you are having difficulty working through in your awakened state.

Father-in-law   If he is in an aggressive state then it is your fear and uncertainty of fitting in and being accepted. If he is loving and accepting then it is you feeling very comfortable with him.

Feet   If your dream focuses on looking down at your own feet you are not dealing with your fear; apprehension and uncertainty; fear of moving forward.

Fire   Indicative of cleansing, growth and change.

Fish   Movement and directional change.

Flatulence   Releasing, letting go old ideas and thought patterns; the acceptance of internal health and well-being.

Flying   Flying can mean going through an astral projection where you are climbing very high out of your physical body; that you are achieving a goal that you have set for yourself; that you're attaining or achieving something somebody else has expected of you.

Food   Preparation of food is significant of cultivating creativity and direction in life. Eating it can be either worrying about weight or accepting the way one looks.

Fortress   A fortress or castle-like environment is significant of needing to be protected from oneself, from others or from life.

Furniture   More furniture than you know what to do with is significant of being overloaded in your home environment, that you need to spring clean. If the furniture is sparse, the house is empty, then it's you feeling unsupported, lacking comfort or being sorry for yourself.

Gambling   This one's not hard—taking a chance on something in your life.

Games   Testing your own or another's confidence in a situation or circumstance; test of skill.

Gates   Something is going out of your life and something is coming in if the gate is swinging back and forth. If the gate is locked up and chained, then you are being stubborn and not allowing something to come into your life. A wide open gate means accepting what is on offer.

Graveyard   Seeing yourself walking through a graveyard may mean that you are reminiscing about a lost relative or that you are feeling very lonely and isolated at the present time. Seeing yourself being buried is significant of you feeling totally weighed down by whatever is going on in your life, by people, situations, circumstances. (*see* Death)

Groups of people   Fear of being taken for granted or used and abused. This can also relate to your property being used and abused, perhaps your sister/brother borrowing clothes.

Hair   Long and flowing reflects self-esteem, short and ratty reflects a lack of belief in self.

Halls and corridors   Getting in touch with deep-seated fears and uncertainties, confusions, difficulties, problems.

Hands   On their own in the dark are representative of inner frustration and confusion; clapping hands reflect inner joy and excitement; handcuffed hands are symbolic of feeling imprisoned in an attitude or a frame of mind or of somebody else imprisoning you with their beliefs and expectations. Open hands mean something is being shown to you in its true form and you are looking at it truly, not through rose-coloured glasses. Closed hands mean that the truth of a situation is hidden from you and you need to be more assertive to find the truth. Dirty hands reflect looking at something you don't want to do but feel compelled to do—loss of free will or a feeling of peer pressure. Clean hands mean you have a job or task you find distasteful (to do or just finished).

Hats   Very significant if they are large and bright, meaning you want to show off or be seen. If they are small and petite you want to be in similar situations or circumstances as others. Very appropriate just before you go for a rise in pay or after a job promotion or new position.

Heaven   Significant of justice, success.

Heirlooms   Family heirlooms are significant of expectation or desire, of goods and chattels that you want to buy, of something of great significance or value to you of a personal nature.

Hell   Significant of the belief that you have done something wrong and are going to be punished for it. Self-punishment or punishment by others. If the flames are being extinguished, you believe that you do not deserve the punishment you feel you're being given.

Hens Hens laying eggs signify wealth and gain, money coming your way; hens barren of eggs represent a fear of losing, the loss of an emotional relationship or a purging of self.

Hole Feeling that you are going into something with anticipation of loss of control, relating to change and direction.

Holiday Travelling or directing yourself wherever you want to go is very symbolic of you being very much in control of your life and its direction.

Holy/religious dream Seeing Jesus, a spiritual or angelic being is very significant of concerns or worry around death which could relate to yourself or someone close to you. It also reflects sorrow that you haven't released relating to a situation in your life.

Home In a house, symbolic of security and balance; the building of a house is significant of you directing yourself in life.

Horse (white) Attraction of money and fertility. Very propitious for a woman trying to achieve pregnancy.

Imposition When you dream that someone is imposing on you it is very significant of you not standing up for yourself in some life situations, of being taken for granted, or being taken advantage of.

Injury Dreaming of an injury to the lower part of the body represents you harming or hurting yourself, of an injury to the upper part of the body represents others inflicting pain or punishment on you. Injuries around the head are symbolic of stimulation and creativity. Eye injury is significant of one not looking at the facts or a life situation as it is. Extreme bleeding is significant of change, of the inner person flourishing.

Insects Symbolic of petty issues driving you crazy. Larger flying insects are symbolic of an attitude problem that someone else has which you can't get home to them. Large, slow moving, sluggish insects reflect you feeling as if you have over-eaten or over-indulged in some pleasurable experience.

Jewellery Tarnished jewellery is normally significant of one's fears or uncertainties and is relevant to money coming into your life. Shiny jewellery represents self-confidence.

Junk Junk piling up in the home or the environment symbolises the fact that you're not doing anything with some or any situation relevant to you. You're allowing things to accumulate without cleaning up. It would be very relevant to someone who is half-hearted about the projects they attack, where the project doesn't meet their expectation levels, simply because they are not putting enough into it.

Karma If we dream about karma we often feel as if we have done something wrong. It can be a precognitive focus of awareness, to reflect that we have just released a karmic debt or cleared out a karmic lesson.

Kiss A very large emotional kiss is significant of being embraced, nurtured and cared for. A little putter of a smooch is relevant to ignoring or dismissing something of no consequence.

Kite Flying high—happiness and success.

Knife Knives are symbolic of a feeling of being stabbed in the back; people are talking about you behind your back; there are secretive discussions going on that you are not involved in.

Knitting Knitting something that is extremely long and drawn-out and tiresome, means we are persevering with a job that we hate and detest. If the knitting is short it means that we are advancing and moving higher (becoming more entwined) in our work environment.

Ladder Climbing with difficulty is stretching oneself beyond one's limits. Racing up a ladder is achievement, reaching one's goals.

Laughter Joyous laughter is excitement and change, excitement and harmony, balance in one's life. Outbursts of laughter, someone else laughing at you.

Letterbox An empty letterbox—normally waiting for something that hasn't arrived, or waiting to hear from someone. Overflowing mail, perhaps being rained on, is significant of the fear you won't receive correspondence from a loved one. A bright red letter box is very significant of receiving money. A white letterbox reflects feelings of being lost, normally the subconscious getting us in touch with our own stored memories and fears and helping us release them and clear them out.

Letters   Receiving letters is significant of a prosperous change coming up in your life. Outgoing mail normally means bills that you have to pay.

Lovers   Attracting someone into one's life. Meeting someone in the astral in an out-of-body experience who would like to come into your life—as opposed to a subconscious dream.

Marriage   Dreaming of your marriage to someone you don't know reveals fear of getting involved or committing yourself. If the marriage is with someone you know, but who seems to be different to the way you know them, then you are afraid of what you are getting into. If the marriage is with the person you love and adore, then it is accepting success and growth. A friend's wedding is significant of an expectation for someone else. Someone else marrying the person you want to be with is significant of holding onto old loves.

Milk   Milk from a cow is significant of motherhood and abundance. Milk from a jug is significant of self-proclaimed wealth and success, self-sufficiency and satisfaction.

Mining   Mining for gold is looking for ideas, looking for understanding, the right job, the right house.

Mirrors   Broken mirrors are symbolic of your beliefs being questioned by others, or of you questioning/comparing others' beliefs with your own. They also reflect the shattering of an illusion or an awakening. Unbroken mirrors are significant of acceptance of other people and of oneself.

Moon   Dreaming of the moon indicates a flash of inspiration, success, money growth, inheritance. In a woman it can represent a period of fertility, in a man a heightened period of creativity and inspiration.

Moss   (*see* Horse)

Moths and butterflies   The more vibrant the colour of the butterfly or moth, the more prosperous and successful you may be; darker or more camouflaged creatures signify success without recognition. They can also represent loss of money or the fear of losing money and/or being out-of-pocket.

Mother-in-law   If she is in an aggressive state then it is your fear and uncertainty of fitting in and being accepted. If she is more loving and accepting then it is you feeling very comfortable with her.

Moving scenery   Dreams involving scenery are symbolic of the need to be on your own, to find peace with yourself, growth and change in your awareness, ideas and perception. Can be significant of being overcrowded in life, at work or at home, or significant of desire for travel or potential travel coming up.

Music   Music frequently represents an out-of-body experience, astral projection or a past-life recall. If you are musically minded it can be significant of a composition that is coming up for you. It also represents the clarity that you have coming forward for you now in this current lifetime to assist you in whatever you are doing and striving for.

Needles and pins   Symbolic of nitpicking and digging for something that you know is ridiculous.

Neighbours   Dreaming of neighbours can signify either problems that may be festering with people you live by or near, or neighbourhood harmony and accepting other people in their own environment.

Nightwear   Coloured nightwear is significant of inner peace and harmony. Dark and reflecting clothing is not wanting to be seen as you are. Striped or spotted nightwear reflects wanting attention from others.

Nose   If your nose seems very large and broad it is directing you towards gain and attainment. A small nose is stimulating growth and change in your money situation, anticipating prosperity and success. A large and runny nose is significant of knowing something but not being able to say anything, a secret significant of challenge and success.

Odour   Very significant of a dental problem that needs attention.

Pain   Symbolic of the release of deep-seated emotions or fears in a situation where you are feeling judged by others.

Palm tree   Money, gain and attitude change for growth.

Pearls   Pearls represent teardrops. They normally mean that we're going through some grief process or a fear of being emotional.

Penis   If a woman is dreaming of a penis she may be very frustrated or have been aroused by or very attracted to a member of the opposite sex. From a man's perspective it could reflect feelings of one-upmanship or of someone stepping over him.

Performing on stage   Seeing yourself on stage performing means that you're not being yourself. You are projecting an image of what you believe others think you should be and you're being judged on that false image. The dream in symbolism is telling you that you feel that you're unable to be yourself, that you have to perform for people and live up to their expectations.

Phone   Expectation or waiting on information or data; past-life recall coming up and preparing itself for recognition.

Pointing fingers   Symbolises feeling imposed on by others or that a situation has finally been resolved in its true order. We're feeling as if we are being judged in a situation unfairly and where we are judging ourselves unfairly.

Policeman   Symbolises money, wealth coming through the family. Inheritance. Concern over legal matters, fear of consequences of your own actions.

Pregnancy   A belief in fertility and growth. Inner fears being unravelled.

Quality   When nothing but the best will do is symbolic of you not accepting less than you believe you deserve.

Radiation   Symbolic of exposure to something that you are unhappy about.

Raunchiness   Having excessive energy and not knowing what to do with it.

Reflections   Reflection of yourself in water or a mirror represents unsuccessfully trying to come to terms with how you feel. Great difficulty with dealing with one's emotions, grief or loss. Reflections of other people mean we are in a wishful frame of mind, looking at our hopes and dreams. Also significant of melancholy.

Relatives   Seeing past relatives popping up in dreams is symbolic of past-life recall, as well as of you reliving an experience that they have had before you.

Ring   Symbolic of coming together, of union or success in relationships or work, or the work and change around oneself.

Rooms   Symbolic of the integration of good health and balance within oneself or in people we may be concerned about. Large and airy rooms signify acceptance that there is more for us to learn, absorb and understand. Small, tight rooms are normally dreamed about by students overburdened by study.

Sacrifice   Sacrifice is the feeling that you have to let something go for someone else's prosperity. It may also reflect bitterness, anger, resentment, an unquenchable appetite, or looking for something you can't find.

School   Feeling you are back at school is feeling as if you have to learn or understand more. Teaching others means you've grown and want to share your knowledge. Being taught by others is significant of inner imbalance, maybe with a health problem. Tormenting others is the beginning of change and strength and determination.

Shadows   Seeing your own shadow means you are feeling exposed and very vulnerable; revealing a dislike of one's body structure; or a fear that you are not being accepted by others. The shadow of someone or something else means you are out of touch with what you want in life and unable to see what is being presented to you by others.

Shepherd   Guardian of the flock. Protector of your spirit.

Silver coins   A small silver coin is symbolic of money coming your way through a lottery win or some other gain, perhaps on the horses. A large silver coin represents inspiration and new ideas, or the need for spring cleaning or instigating changes in one's life.

Smiling faces   Clearing and change. Acceptance, inner harmony and balance.

Snakes   Snakes and serpents and all small venomous animals that are frightening represent a belief that somebody is talking about you or that you're not involved in a situation others are involved in. You feel left out, judged or condemned for a situation. You feel that people don't understand you properly. It also represents the fact that you are not voicing your opinion properly and you are doing it in your dream state.

Snakes and serpents, reptiles of any description, may also represent a conflict with another person in which you feel their personality is overriding yours. Their belief about what you should do is different from your own. You can't please someone. You're unable to behave in a way that they want you to behave or they behave in a way that is foreign to you and you can't deal with. In other words they're not being the person you feel they should be.

Snow or ice   Very symbolic of fear or apprehension. Clarity in its purest form, inspiration and change. Cleansing of the body and mind. Very spiritual.

Sounds   Sharp sounds, very distracting, represent conflict and confusion.

Spiders   Large and darkly coloured spiders are significant of prosperity, the beginning of change, something coming into your life after a famine or a feast. When you have gone through a period where money seems to have gone out the window it's coming back in to you through the symbolism of the spider. The bigger the spider the more relevant it is to the amount of money you've got. If you see yourself squashing the spider it is important that you redo an affirmation the next day affirming that you accept the gift that it was offering you and release any fear that you may have had relating to it. If you have any fear attached, then acknowledge that you choose to release the fear and accept the gift on offer.

A spider with a red back is significant of you receiving something with a price. A spider with a yellow stripe means receiving something, but you actually have to work at something to receive it. Mottled or other colorations are significant of you not seeing the gift as clearly as it is offered to you—you are not aware of the purpose of the gift. A purple or lavender hue around the spider is representative of it being a spiritual gift; it may be an offering from your guide.

Stains   Stains reflect finickiness, perhaps about stains on clothes, something you can't remove or be rid of.

Stars   Stars shining brightly are about ideas and concepts being awakened and opened up. Very dim, tiny stars are significant of difficulty with eyesight or headaches.

Stones/Gems   (*see* Appendix B—Crystals)

Teeth   New teeth coming in represent wisdom and discovery, self-awareness, inner peace and a spiritual path opening up to you.

Trees   Bright coloured but sparse trees are significant of creativity or the attraction of change in your life. Deep dark rich colours are significant of spiritual unfolding or awakening in awareness and self-discovery.

Tunnels   Dark endless tunnels reflect never finding what one is looking for. Short, blocked tunnels represent understanding coming forth.

Umbrellas   Preparation for change, preparing for a heavy or extra work load. Also significant of emotions being released and opened up.

Untidiness   Very significant of being overtired or overloaded.

Victory   A reflection of the stimulation of achieving a goal.

Virtue   Signifying that you have lived up to your own beliefs and expectations.

Vulnerability   Once again, a feeling of being exposed or open to other people's ridicule. (*see* Being exposed)

Wager/Bet   Seeing yourself placing a bet on a situation means that you are unsure of being successful.

Walls Significant of obstacle and restrictions.

Wandering Feeling tired or exhausted, frustrated and fed up.

War An accumulation of war wounds, memory; release of emotions; the annihilation of an arch rival.

Water Water washing something away means that some hard work is finished and over, coming into a more balanced time. Swift-flowing water—change, one you can't keep up with. Rivers and waterfalls represent cleansing. It means that you're either destroying or releasing a part of your life that was dysfunctional and you're moving into new things, totally releasing the past and cleansing yourself of it. When you see yourself in a pleasant water environment it means that you're growing and moving forward. You're very happy and balanced in that movement. You feel confident in your potential level of achievement.

Wine cellar Significant of storage of prized goods or belongings.

Xenophobia In the dream state relates to fear of travel.

Yappiness Again, somebody gossiping behind your back.

Yarn/Story Hearing somebody spreading a yarn about somebody else is very significant of the fear that people are talking behind your back.

Zebra crossing Moving obstacles out of one's path.

Zippers A zipper stuck open represents exposure in a situation where you are not quite finished something you're working on. A zipper fully done up means that you are ready to show or perform in a work situation. A short zipper means you don't have enough material for something that you are working on; a too-long zipper means you have overestimated a situation.

Zodiacal signs Significant of the integration and acceptance of many people in your life.

Zoo Feeling as if people are driving you crazy or work situations are overloading you.

Dream analysis

How do we analyse our dreams? Dreams are very important to life generally. We dream subconscious thoughts about our daily activities. We dream about our ambitions, our hopes. We dream about our expectations, things we would like to have happen, or about things that are problems for us. Dreams are the mind's way of keeping us sane and functional and helping us learn to cope with everything we deal with on a daily basis.

Every dream is important, even the ones we don't remember. Some dreams we don't remember because we are not at a point where we are ready to take responsibility for whatever is concerning us, or because our subconscious is just rehashing all the different experiences that we have had. They are not in a particular structure for us to look at so we're actually just filing all this data and getting it ready to surface in our dream state at a later stage.

People frequently dream in black and white; generally these dreams are dealing with current issues, and are normally in that format.

We dream in colour when our need is to have clarity about all parts of our dream. In other words, we want to remember all of it, not just bits of it. The colour gives us more focus, more conscious memory of what our dream has been. We bring it up in colour to fit into the structure of whatever we're dealing with at the current time. When we're expanding or opening up to new things, we dream in colour and actually bring forward memories of past-life experiences to assist us with our current direction in life.

We wake up very refreshed and clear minded from our dream state when we have actually looked at something in our lives and resolved it. When we wake up feeling confused it means that the issue is still relevant and we're not sure how to deal with it, so by a continuation of different dreams we give ourselves the extra data that we need to resolve the experience.

Sometimes we wake up from a dream feeling that it was so real it must be something that is going to happen; this is a false fear. If the dream was a little frightening and we have woken feeling as if the dream was reality, we must remember that our dreams are very symbolic and may not represent exactly what we see in a dream state. Sometimes our symbolism is frightening.

When we awaken frightened from a dream it means that we have a fear in our physical reality. All our dream is doing is trying to show us that we have a fear that we are not working with or resolving. It is trying to give us clarity to support us in what we are trying to do.

Dreams are very prophetic. They give us the opportunity of assisting ourselves in our awakened state—in our lives, in our expansion, in our growth. By keeping a record of our dreams and reviewing them perhaps a month or two later, we'll see a sequence of patterns forming—the same applies to our daily awakened state.

If you record what is going on in your life during your wakened state as well as in your dream state, you will see how they fit together. This will give you greater insight into understanding yourself, where you are limiting yourself, where your concerns are. I find it's wonderfully helpful to keep a notepad or tape near your bed so that on awakening from a dream you can record it as quickly as possible before it's lost. Do an affirmation before you go to sleep at night—just mentally focus with deep breathing and ask that you be able to remember and store with clarity any dream that you have during the night. Keep affirming it and it will start to happen. Everybody dreams, the difficulty is just allowing yourself to have memory of your thoughts. Dreams are very important tools in our lives. Let's use them.

Creating a dream workbook

When you start recording your dreams in your workbook, it is important to keep a diary of some sort of the things that are going on in your life so that you can more easily compare your dreams with what is happening in your physical, awakened state. It may also give you the keys to unlocking your individual symbolism. This can be accomplished in the same book—see the example on the following page.

After you have recorded your dreams for a period of, let's say, two weeks to a month to begin with, get a notebook and record your dreams in sequence daily. Make an alphabetical index of your dream symbols in the back of the book. All this data becomes a manual of your own dream symbology. Patterns will begin to emerge as you see what each symbol means to you individually.

List what all the symbols represent to you. Cats, for example: black cats jumping on you in a dream mean that you're not looking at something, not resolving an issue or refusing to take notice of something that is affecting you—and you're wallowing in the effect of it. Cats moving around you or in your environment generally mean an awakening of your own spiritual growth, your sensitivity, that you're coming into a focus of knowledge and understanding. To see a cat and be very frightened of it means that you're frightened of what you're seeing in yourself. Seeing a cat in a fight represents a tug of war you're having with yourself, an imbalance in your decision-making.

After putting your symbols together over a two-week period you will find they begin to make sense to you and the dream patterns fall in place. You will find from recording the symbols that you are able to analyse the dream; that you can do this even better once you have compiled the index of the meaning of your symbols. Remember that there can be more than one meaning to a symbol; just as our ideas change, personal symbolic meanings can also change.

Before going further go over the period of dreams and see if there is a change in the dream structure from beginning to end. Date your dream record so that you can keep a dated order from month to month and then compile your manual.

Sample dream workbook

Date: _____

Dream:

Second night in a row I dreamed that a large orange cat was sitting next to the right front tyre of my car.

Awakened Day:

Clothes worn:
White shirt, black tie, black slacks, black socks/shoes.

Events:

Had an argument with co-worker over who was responsible for counting blue widgets. She went to my supervisor who said I was to count the blue ones and she was to count the red ones. The co-worker made me mad because I got in trouble with the supervisor.

Had flat tyre on the way home from work, noticed it was low for the past few days but didn't pay any attention to it.

Comments:

Should have paid attention to the cat in the dream the first night and I wouldn't have had the flat on the way home.

Watch for tonight's dream or one within a few days to reflect something concerning the unresolved personal conflict at work (snakes, serpents, or small venomous animals.)

Ten steps to understanding your dreams

1. Recalling the dream

How can you determine what type of dream you are having? Because one tends to forget the contents of a dream very soon after awakening, you should immediately record the dream on paper or on a small tape recorder kept next to the bed. Later in the day, or at the end of the week, you can check back on the dreams to see which of the three categories each one fits into. Another technique that is helpful in remembering dreams is to make an affirmation just before bedtime that you wish to remember any dream that occurs during the night. If you wake up after a dream, record it immediately, don't wait till the next morning.

a. Recording the dream provides future reference for dream patterns.

b. Methods—paper and pen or (better) a tape recorder.

c. Time frame—it is important to do it as soon as you wake.

d. Details—record the dream in as much detail as you can remember.

2. Defining the type of dream

Out-of-body, subconscious, daydream, et cetera.

3. Structure of the dream

Historic, current or future.

4. Effect of the dream

What kind of feelings did you have on awakening?

5. Specific symbols

Cats, falling, snakes, gems, flying, etcetera.

6. Dream analysis

Use the guidelines given here to analyse your dream.

7. Recurring dreams

a. Same dream—recurrent dreams mean unresolved issues. What are they?

b. Dream continuation—your subconscious is trying to make a point on a particular issue.

8. Concurrent dreams with another person

Mutual thoughts of each other prior to sleep so you make a connection in the astral.

9. Effects of another person's dream on you

This is the interlinking of astral bodies discussed earlier.

10. Using your gut-level instincts

Paying attention to that 'little voice within you' which is, in fact, your 'lower self' or instinctive mind or intuitive subconscious.

CHAPTER 4

Colour

The colour spectrum seen in dreams also relates to the auric and etheric fields of energy that surround us. The seven major energy centres each vibrate at a specific rate which is the same frequency which generates or causes us to see the colour attributed to that centre, red, orange, yellow, green, blue, indigo and violet.

These energy centres work on creating balance and harmony within our body. We are energy, we give energy, we breathe energy. If life is balanced then these energy centres or chakras are balanced. If we have difficulties in life then our centres become blocked or restricted. When we clear our problems up we release these restrictions and go back to a total balance. When we are in total balance then we have an auric field that reflects the entire colour spectrum.

Colour is very important in our dreams, but we rarely dream in just pure-coloured symbolism. Rather, a dream may feature a predominant colour in clothes or furniture or surroundings. Colour is the key to understanding our dream state, and to understand our symbology we need to understand what our colours represent. The more you take notice of your dreams and record them the more clearly you will recall them and the more aware you will be of the colours, the symbols, the structure of your dreams, how they form, how they shape.

Black or a murky brown in a dream represents great confusion or anxiety. It can be a warning that you should take stock of your situation and really look at what you're doing at the present time. It also means that you're feeling overwhelmed by your circumstances or situation and there is a need for time out to reflect and re-evaluate why you are feeling the way you do. It can also represent depression. The body's health status can dictate that we dream in these colours; if you are on antibiotics or other forms of drugs the chemical reaction in your body can actually bring up a brownish-blackish type of dream—purely an effect of the drugs.

Dreaming in black and white is quite a different thing. We normally dream in black and white when we are choosing not to remember dreams; or when our subconscious is trying to infiltrate some awareness into the dream state and giving it to us in black and white. Black and white can also represent the way a person thinks. If we think more than feel then we can have black and white dreams because we are not comfortable with the colours of emotion. That is, we dream in black and white because we are thinking, not feeling, and our dreams are reflecting our thoughts, pure thought.

Grey in a dream represents obstruction—a situation that is just unattainable, a problem to which you can't quite get the answer.

Colour is very significant in the healing of the physical body. Dreaming in colour is balancing our thinking and our feeling so that our body will go through a recovery period while we're asleep and be fit and well to deal with life situations as they come up throughout our lives. (Colour is discussed further in Appendix A, pp.103–120.)

Colours in dreams

Red

Red can represent a deep emotion or strongly blocked problem. It can represent the body going through a healing process. It can also mean that the person has a lot of physical energy—is very active and very physical. It can relate to sensual experience, sexual fantasies. It also relates to personal fulfilment. In dreams red can signify that someone is very attractive to someone else. It can also represent a warning, depending on the depth of the colour. The deeper and more prevalent the red in the dream the more it can represent concerns on an emotional level, an uncertainty about the attraction being mutual, or being overwhelmed by a feeling of love.

Red is also a way of releasing emotion. Through your dream you are actually letting go of your feelings, feelings that you may be having difficulty with in your wakened state.

Red is symbolic of hope, of the opportunity for success. If it is related in the dream to career or work, it also structures concerns and worries—the deeper the red the stronger your concern. The lighter or brighter the red the more balanced you feel about the situation. If you were to see red in an abstract dream that was a little bit frightening, that would mean that you have some concerns and your subconscious is trying to show you so in an abstracted form so that you don't ignore the problem. If you're not concerned about something in a work environment, all the dream is doing is reminding you that you have concerns or anxieties about something.

Red toned down to a very soft gentle pink would mean you are getting excited. Perhaps you are coming up for promotion or there is potential for growth in your career or a relationship.

In its lighter shades, red is potential success. It is a striving colour, indicating moving forward, expanding, opening up to situations, promoting a successful outcome. In its darker shades it represents the fact that you are striving, you wish to succeed but you have reservations, your own confidence base is not secure. Perhaps external influences are concerning you, that is, the way people perceive you.

Orange

Orange represents the level of storage where we store our emotions and feelings, rather than the actual facts of a situation. (That happens at a higher level.) Orange is significant of how things have affected you. It represents a need for some form of meditation or exercise that will eliminate nervous energy, that is, it represents stored nervous energy or anxieties, feelings and emotions, being a signal to the body that these stored feelings could have an effect on your health.

To dream in orange means your body is trying to tell you that it needs to be looked at, that something is creating an imbalance in your system. It could signify the onset of a virus that the body is preparing to fight. It could signify that you are run-down, running on nervous energy, and that it's time to take stock in your life.

Orange could also be a warning that a situation coming up is not going to be as successful as you would like it to be, that there are going to be problems with the way you deal with that situation. It's telling you that perhaps your anxieties and concerns will put you in a position where you deal with a situation wrongly. It's giving you a chance to re-evaluate, time out to think about your approach in any given situation.

Yellow/Gold

Gold signifies great opportunity and success. Gold in the career area represents an expansion in the direction you are taking in your career path. It would show that you had great confidence and self-assertiveness and were very sure that you were in the right position at the right time. If the gold dream was pre-empting this situation it would be saying you are going to be very successful, you are going to achieve great things, you are making the right choice for yourself at this point.

Yellow represents subconscious thinking. It's bringing up the mental activity of the day, the week, month or year. It's unravelling all the different types of experiences you deal with through your life. It's amplifying the clarity of these situations. You are ticking them over in your mind and you are aware of them, you're putting them in their rightful perspective and you are dealing with them. So it's telling you you're moving forward with anything you're dealing with subconsciously or consciously. You are in the right frame of mind and you are attacking life with the right approach or emphasis.

Just like the sun shining, yellow says that you are in harmony with yourself and your life and life situations.

Green

An emotional colour. Appearing as a lush, vibrant colour, green is telling you that you are in love with life, your position in life, with friends and loved ones. You are in emotional balance with yourself and other people. It's amplifying good health and vitality in your body and your emotional outlook on life.

In deeper shades green signifies jealousies or uncertainties about what other people are saying or what you believe other people are thinking. It's the colour of confrontation. It normally puts you in a position to clarify such situations. It's an amplification of the mind being expansive in its general view so that you are able to perceive not only your own perspective but other people's. It gives you great balance in the decisions that you make in life.

Blue

The communication colour. It represents great clarity and the ability to voice any situation well. It signifies an alignment with the other colours which means you are in balance with your life. An excellent colour to be dreaming with when communication is important.

Indigo

Indigo represents thought. It is where we self-analyse how we feel generally. It can signify our restlessness with life and our quest for more spiritually-minded activities. It's a searching colour looking for more or new directions in life, at the need to enhance our abilities, to re-evaluate the direction that we're taking in life and to look at what we want to do with life. It's an expansive mental colour, a very reflective colour on life and its situations.

Violet

Violet goes beyond indigo into awareness. Having expanded we now have an understanding of what we want to incorporate in our lives. It is a colour for the quest of life, taking on new challenges, adding new directions, actioning changes with great clarity. It is a colour for clarity and understanding in all issues of life.

When we dream in this colour, we are expanding and opening up our total form. We perceive and know what we are, how we affect other people, what is necessary in life, what gives us great joy and happiness. It is a balancing colour. It is harmonious with self-awareness and being in tune with oneself.

Colour around us

Red

1. Meditation   Meditating in a red atmosphere stimulates energy, expands the physical vitality of the body and awakens the mind to clarity and expansion for an invigorating meditation. Red also opens our awareness of our emotional status, it allows us to recognise how our body is dealing with stress or general day-to-day concerns.

2. Surroundings   Red in room decoration and in the clothes you wear can have some surprising subliminal effects. Red is a very stimulating colour in all its shades, from light, lustrous rosy pink to dark burgundy. The effect of red in a bedroom is disastrous. Here the stimulation of the colour during your sleeping hours activates restless sleep and deep and tiring thought patterns. You would find you arose either extremely tired and lethargic or 'super hyper', unable to slow down all day. It's one extreme or the other. In a lounge room it stimulates conversation but in a dining room it stimulates appetite, perhaps making you eat too quickly and creating indigestion problems.

Red clothes can generate a higher level of energy—which works wonderfully well with someone who has just recovered from the flu. It is also a good colour to wear when we need to be assertive; it is a self-confident colour. The wearer of red is always seen to be very much in control of the situation. It also attracts people to you in a very friendly and trusting way. A businessperson would be wise to wear a dark suit, white shirt and red tie or scarf when conducting social-type business meetings in the evening.

Orange

1. Meditation   Meditating in an orange atmosphere inhibits pain. I once went through an entire dental session having a tooth capped—drilling the hole for a pin to hold the new cap with an exposed nerve—with no novocaine or other painkillers except that I meditated in a bright orange atmosphere a very long way away from my mouth and the dental surgery. Orange is also said to stimulate the appetite. (How many restaurants use an orange interior?) Orange generates healing and balance to the physical form; it works on promoting oxygen into the body, allowing calmness and serenity while meditating. It also clears the mind of confusion and allows us focus and clarity while in meditation.

2. Surroundings   The subliminal effect of orange in room decoration and in the clothes are mixed. Orange is a very unusual colour to have in a bedroom but with the new colour prints it seems to be becoming more popular. Blended in with other colours like blue or green it balances the effect out in bedlinen but on its own its effects are similar to those of red. It also works with stimulation and although it can have very positive healing properties, to have it close to you in bed creates a need to wrestle with your problems, not just the day-to-day ones but the ones you have avoided and don't really know what to do with. It brings up a lot of past memories so your sleep can be disturbed by the turbulence of a collection of mixed emotions, running from birth to the present; as well, a lot of recall back to birth and for some, into past-life recall, can be brought up. The mixture of issues from your past inevitably creates confusion.

Orange is, however, a lovely colour in the kitchen or brunch area as it stimulates communication and can help the cook with focus—but there is a negative side once again. You could end up worrying so much about your culinary efforts that you burn the dinner!

Orange is a very heavy colour to wear unless you are going through a recovery period; then it stimulates the immune system and can help revitalise the body's energy.

Yellow

1. Meditation   Meditating in a yellow atmosphere increases the heart rate and respiration and stimulates the left side of the brain, the side which controls such things as judgment, writing skills, reasoning, logic and right-hand movements. It allows our deep subconscious programming to rise during meditation and help us consciously look at our problems, how we are burying them and what our fears and uncertainties are in life.

2. Surroundings   The subliminal effects of yellow in room decoration and clothing are generally positive. Yellow is a lovely colour for a child's room. It stimulates balance and harmony and can enhance the resolve and issues that a child deals with. In an adult's bedroom it creates overactivity in the subconscious, which promotes a lot of very abstract and perhaps even weird and strange dreams, once again very tiring to awaken from.

In clothing yellow is a thoughtful colour; it can assist us in opening up new ideas and clearing out old programming and thought patterns. It can also be a very stimulating colour in clothing, working well with stimulating ideas and thoughts as well as being excellent for energy; in any physical task you need to take on yellow will give you an added surge of energy.

Green

1. Meditation   Meditating in a green atmosphere allows the body and mind to heal and balance themselves. It has a calming effect on our senses without the use of drugs. Its relaxing effects are wonderful for a woman trying to conceive, to focus on through her system, not only relaxing her mind and body and preparing it for the fertile period of ovulation but also generating an increase in her fertility potential. Green has long been known as a healing colour.

2. Surroundings   The subliminal effects of green in one's surroundings are all beneficial. If you're decorating with green use a variety of shades to create harmony, but not too much green overall as you can find it makes you so relaxed you may only want to sleep—blue is much more uplifting. Green is very beneficial to migraine sufferers.

Green is one of my favourite colours for bedsheets; it creates balance and helps you to relax, to release your awakened thought pattern and have a very restful sleep. It also regenerates your energy balance so you awake feeling light, refreshed and full of energy. It is a lovely colour for a child's room, making the child feel safe, secure and in balance with itself and secure in its environment. In the bathroom it's conducive to refreshing the individual. In the kitchen it stimulates your creativity and in the dining room it helps aid in the digestion of your meal. This colour in clothing is extremely stimulating for one's creativity—ideas will flow well in this colour, an excellent colour to wear if you utilise your mind in your job. It's also an excellent colour to attract a rise in pay as your boss will appreciate your productivity, as well as, perhaps, your promotional potential.

Blue

1. Meditation   Meditating in a blue atmosphere—blue is one of the best colours for relaxation, especially light blue. (Pale blue and pale pink are both very calming colours.)

Blue expands our consciousness, creates harmony and balance in the body, heals and nurtures the muscular structure of the body, allowing it to relax properly and enjoy its time of rest during meditation. It also expands the clarity of our consciousness, opening the mind to new concepts and ideas.

2. Surroundings   The subliminal effects of blue in room decoration and clothing are very positive. Blue is my other favourite colour; it is wonderful for bedlinen, curtains and walls. Just like the green it balances out the mind and allows you to have a peaceful night's sleep; it comforts the mind so the body relaxes and deep sleep is what it allows you. In any room in the house it creates a feeling of harmony. It will assist study in the child's room and concentration in the other rooms of the home.

Blue is a lovely colour to wear, promoting balance and harmony. You would feel very secure in yourself and directional in this colour. It is an excellent colour to use when you need to communicate with others as well as being a wonderful colour for a speaker. Worn in a work environment it would be a colour worn by someone who appears to get on well with people, a good communicator.

Indigo

1. Meditation   Mediating in an indigo atmosphere allows our psychic awareness to expand, helping us focus on concepts beyond our normal level of understanding. By doing this we are able to encapsulate understanding with new work concepts and projects. It also allows us a broader understanding of physical and spiritual matters.

2. Surroundings Indigo is not a suitable colour for bedlinen or decor. It has very spiritual qualities and yet is an extremely heavy colour to relate to in an environment. A person wearing indigo has difficulty relating to everyday areas of their lives. Instead, their focus is on future thought patterns, thinking ahead and daydreaming. This colour is normally worn when you are soul-searching.

Violet

1. Meditation Meditating in a violet atmosphere encompasses all our feelings and emotions and gives us an expansion of empathy for others, helping us understand their point of view as well as our own. It enables us to see much more of the total picture rather than just the periphery of our own feelings. In meditation it calms our consciousness so we can grasp the understanding that we are searching for; in other words, it allows us to ask our deepest, darkest question or look at our worst fear and accommodate it with an answer. Violet stimulates deep thought patterns and once again spiritual awareness; it is a good colour for deep meditation by the adept.

2. Surroundings The subliminal effects of violet in room decoration and clothing are mixed. Violet in its softest shades, very pale, is a lovely colour in a child's bedroom, as well as in an adult's bedroom—it helps with memories of your dreams and life experiences. As well as soothing the body and the mind into gentle calming sleep, pale violet is a calm and relaxing colour on the body and mind. I would not use a darker shade as it tends to block memory instead, creating the effect of oversleep. On awakening you would find that dark violet's effects are extremely tiring on you and your day is one spent trying to wake up. In other rooms it can create a listless feeling.

CHAPTER 5

Self-help Techniques and Alternatives

The sleep state takes you sequentially through various levels of sleep during the night. You fall first into a very deep sleep (theta or delta level), and then you slowly come back up to the alpha state, which is very light sleep. At this level you are very susceptible to subliminal suggestions. If you had a subliminal tape running, you would gain the most benefit from it in the beta state because then you are opening your subconscious thinking, where you bring up all the stored data that you're not relating to in a conscious state. It's like reviewing your day's activities. It's a time when your mind actually activates a collective thought pattern and shows you all the things that have gone on for you. Because your eyes are the main focus of your wakened state they absorb every single thing that you see during the day. Even though you don't consciously register perhaps as much as 70 per cent of what you see, the eyes see everything. They see the finite detail on a wall, the minute detail in the situation that you're in, facial expressions, everything. All this is recorded in your subconscious and when you're asleep your mind releases it. It's as though your mind has collected a whole range of thoughts that are no longer relevant to you and lets them go, then looks at the ones that you're holding on to. If you're not doing anything with them then it stores them at the lower level of the deep subconscious.

Subliminal tapes

When you open up your subconscious during the beta level of sleep you receive all the data that you've collected naturally during the day. Once it is released the subconscious can open to other things, such as a subliminal tape. If the tape was talking about self-confidence and love that would align with anything in your subconscious that was not functioning on that level. Information about reservations and fears on a tape would align with your reservations and fears and would give you access to releasing them. You could extend your dream state because of a subliminal tape, actually come awake feeling very confident about a situation because you've absorbed a tape helping you to feel good about yourself, which would also make you look at any reason why you don't feel good. It activates a very positive change in the way you see yourself.

Subliminal tapes at this level can be very beneficial. People can program themselves for studying, for example. When people have a lot of problems with study, they go into a fear situation where they feel, 'I'm not going to remember any of this, I'm going to do very poorly in my exams,' which can easily become a self-fulfilling prophecy. Subliminal work helps greatly here because it's opening up to a subconscious state without reservation, where you are absorbing all the data you need. You awaken and it's all there, and you find it very easy to retrieve it. While the subliminal tape is running you'd stay in that subconscious state which you activate continuously through the night anyway. You are going up and down through the levels normally, but while you are working with the subliminal you could not have an out-of-body or astral experience. Once the tape finished and your mind had completed whatever it had wanted to release it would still go through its own processes, then you would move on to the other levels, going deeper or higher. If you went deeper then you could leave your body, going into an astral projection. The astral projection would go on its normal course.

Astral projection

You can exist in the astral for a very long period although you're still bound to the earth by your physical body which dictates a need for your presence. Sleep keeps us working through our life experiences. Our conscious mind takes a break during the sleep state but the only times the subconscious can free itself are when we go into an out-of-body experience or an astral projection. Most people just don't have recall of these occurrences unless they make a conscious effort to record the dream immediately upon awakening. Recall happens naturally for those who meditate regularly, as their minds readily register out-of-body experiences. They are much more in touch with their spirit essence and can feel the separation. If you don't meditate, it's very natural for your system to react to the need for astral projection and to project while you're sleeping.

Fear of astral projection is nothing more than fear of an unknown quantity. The thought 'I'm going out of body' could raise a great deal of fear for those who don't recognise they have actually done it many times. One who meditates would recognise the feeling instantly and have no fear. This weird sensation that people talk about really can be quite a scary thought, but it is no more frightening than going to sleep at night. Nothing is going to happen to you. You have natural abilities which your body is responding to. There is a need for separation during sleep where you free yourself from your physical body and have time out. You may just sit in your lounge room and just feel the room you live in. You may go and visit a loved one. You may go higher and have an astral projection to another plane of existence of which you have no recall at all. That's very normal. Probably 99 per cent of the population at one point in their lives have had an out-of-body experience that they can recall, whether they relate it to the status of an astral body projection or not.

Meditation

I've included this section not so much to teach you to mediate but to assist you in increasing your awareness and understanding that meditation helps you to open in the dream state. It is one thing to have an interesting dream, but it is something else altogether to be open to the guidance offered by that dream.

Meditation is a rewarding exercise in harmony and balance. Through meditation we learn how to relax properly and open up our creativity and potential creativity. The benefits of meditation are endless. You can focus and feel good about yourself. It releases stress and anxiety in the body and it stops health problems. It can keep your body functioning at its full potential.

There are many different types of meditation, and some of them are very complex. A lot of people say, 'I just don't have the time to meditate. I don't have the time to sit and chant. I don't have the time to go along to a centre and learn techniques in meditation.' Well, you don't have to. There are very simple techniques that you can apply in your everyday life to achieve a very successful state of meditation. (Meditation is also discussed in Appendix A, page 103.) Firstly you must clear your mind of all thoughts. There are two ways to do this. The first is to listen to some relaxing music—instrumental only, no voices: classical (particularly Baroque) or ambient (New Age), Kitaro, Japanese. The second method is to use a breathing technique.

Let's start with the breathing technique (this can be a meditation in itself). Learn to take very deep breaths. Focus inside your mind, slowly counting to four, take a nice deep breath in through your nose and take it deep down in your abdomen. Hold it for a moment. Again to a count of four, very slowly exhale through your mouth and as you exhale say to yourself, 'Relax. I'm going to let myself relax', and release all the tension and stress built up through the day. 'I'm letting go of all my problems. I'm releasing all my thoughts and all I'm going to do is relax.' Repeat this a minimum of three times; for maximum benefit it is normally recommended that you breathe this way for one to three minutes.

Colour is a very important part of meditation. We can use the focus of the sun. Imagine bright rays of golden sun pouring down over you, washing over your body and gently warming, massaging and relaxing every part of your being. Feel it flowing through your veins to all parts of your body. Just release yourself into this wonderful feeling of light surrounding you and pouring down through your body, cleansing and purifying. In your mind have a focus of cleansing and purifying. You might like to see it as water. See yourself in a watery environment relaxing and just releasing yourself into the water and letting it heal and nurture you. Visualise with the unlimited power of your mind every organ and system within your body as normal and healthy, functioning as it should. You may like to see yourself sitting under a tree in your favourite picnic spot, or on a totally deserted mountaintop, and allow the earth to regenerate your energy. This is called creative visualisation.

This is a wonderful technique for meditation. You can put yourself in any situation. In other words, whatever you imagine becomes your meditation. So open to what you feel you would like to imagine each time you meditate. See yourself on a deserted tropical island, walking through a wonderful rainforest, sitting in a meadow by a cool mountain stream. You may design a room which you decorate and furnish with anything in any colour combination you wish. Money is no object so make it as lavish as you wish. The list is endless. Just open your mind to the total concept of imagination and allow yourself to step into another world, a world free of all the restrictions and limitations of your everyday life. Use your breathing to help you relax. Deep breathing and total relaxation for a short time are a must and may be the totality of the meditation.

After several of these meditation exercises, you may choose to expand the technique and during this relaxed state look at conditions that are causing you problems in reality. Bring them up slowly, one at a time, and look at them *without being emotional or judgmental* as to who is right or wrong. Look at what the problem really is, and work on how you might resolve it so that everyone comes out a winner. Release your emotions, let go of them. This way you are not limiting what you feel. Emotions restrict resolving your problems because you go into pain or anguish which stops you looking at the problems realistically. You go into the feelings instead. So use your breathing and your favourite place or scenery to help you let go and then see the problem for what it is. Try to concentrate on letting it unfold by itself rather than forcing or creating the situation and the outcome. (Mentally creating the situation and the outcome will put you into a daydream, and daydreams will not give you the insight you are seeking.) Look at how you can achieve a goal instead—a successful goal. Use your breathing in harmony with the golden ray of light. Feel it permeating everything around you. When you've finished meditating just seal yourself in a golden bubble for a while and feel relaxed, harmonious, warm and loved.

The other technique of meditation uses music. While you are listening to the music feel the wonderful ray of sunlight washing through you, and focus on your problems. Let the music help you keep your emotions at bay. Release them. Now when you look at the situation which is causing your feelings you can resolve it without the emotions. The emotions settle into balance. You won't feel conflicted by them as before. You no longer have the extreme pain or anguish, but a resolve and a direction to take. You then feel much more relaxed in yourself, harmonious and happy.

Once you learn how to relax with meditation you can do it in a matter of minutes. You can change a stressful situation into a calm and balanced situation, even in your workplace. Once you get into a routine with meditation you don't have to take a lengthy period of time to relax. You'll find that by utilising the techniques you've just learnt—deep breathing, feeling colour or water splashing through you—relaxation is instantaneous. It has a very positive effect because you are changing your mental thought pattern on stress and how to relax and enjoy harmony and balance. You will find it generates an increase in your energy level. You're in a better position then to deal with whatever is going on in your life.

Controlling pain

You can use meditation to release a migraine headache, a tension headache, any type of headache by using a golden ray of light, just washing it through you and letting yourself float off with music. You don't have to have any scenery. You don't have to look at your problems. You can just relax to the music and the lovely golden ray of light, or see yourself floating in water and just relax purely to the music and let it take you away. You are releasing the stress and tension in your body and you are releasing the headache.

The same applies to other types of pain. We can actually control pain. Pain becomes a problem because it tires the body and when the body is tired the pain becomes more extreme than it would have been. Pain is a very localised condition which draws your attention to that specific area. It is actually very simple to take a mental holiday and focus your attention somewhere else.

Using a meditation, a creative visualisation technique to relax yourself, will release the restrictive tension in the body. You are placing less pressure on your body. Relax to the feeling of the sunlight washing through you or see yourself floating freely in the water. See the water washing the pain away. See yourself floating in and out with the tide and as you do feel the pain is releasing. This is a very effective technique.

Another meditation technique for pain is seeing yourself in a snowfield. Very deep in a snowfield. See your whole body lying in a snowfield and feel the cold actually penetrating to where pain is. See it actually numbing the area that is causing pain. Use your breathing to help you release yourself into this environment of snow. Feel the snowflakes falling down and relaxing your body. You are cocooned in a very thick thermal structure except for the part of the body that is causing you pain. You are very warm and comfortable, only exposing that part of your body that is causing you pain to the cold sensation. Let this cold sensation move slowly through that part of your body until the pain is released. Use your breathing to help you relax. Play music if you choose or just float freely without any outside influences. This is a very effective tool for pain management.

The water environment releases body pain as well as headache. See yourself floating in a pool of water or on a beach going in and out with the tide, releasing the pain, the pent-up pressure, into the water, freeing it. Feel the water actually draw the pain out of your body and releasing it. Let go of it. This works very well for asthma, bronchial conditions and congestion in the body as well.

If you're suffering from arthritic or rheumatic conditions you could see yourself floating in a sauna, a very warm sauna. See a very large sponge over the area that is in pain or trauma. Feel the sponge drawing out the pain totally and when the sponge is filled squeeze it into the water. Cleanse it. The water will absorb all the negativity. Then place it back over the area that you want to heal. Feel it once again drawing out the sensation and see yourself getting more flexibility in that part of your body. Use your breathing to help you relax and release any tension or stress.

If you are going into an anxiety attack or a panic attack then just see yourself floating freely in space, cocooned in a bubble of blue light. Focus on your body. See it relaxing. Start from the tips of your toes and see yourself releasing the tension slowly as you move your focus slowly up your body. Feel your pulse rate slowing down, your heartbeat slowing down. You're coming more into focus. Use your breathing to help you relax. Feel the blue light massaging through your body and relaxing you, giving you focus. Feel your breathing become freer and more relaxed. Move this sensation slowly up your body until it gets to the top of your head and feel it massaging and relaxing your scalp. Every part of you will be in harmony and balance. Just relax. Let yourself release the anxiety. Use your breathing to help you—nice slow deep breaths continuously relaxing you.

Affirmations

Affirmations are a very important structure in our lives. We actually affirm every situation in life, but mostly in a negative sense: I can't do this, I won't do that, I'm unable to do this, I can't achieve that, It's an impossible situation, I'll never do it, This will never happen. Each of these statements is correct because you have affirmed them.

We have to learn to change our negative affirmations into positive affirmations. You're setting yourself up for failure with 'I can't' or 'It's an impossible situation'. You don't believe that you are capable of doing something and lose the momentum of actually achieving it because you already doubt the outcome. You don't see yourself achieving. You have to change this into a positive outlook by setting a goal and by continually affirming it: 'I can and will achieve it.' If you put momentum into yourself and promote positive energy, you will move in a positive direction.

Affirmations are tools to utilise in everyday life. The reason you affirm in the negative is that you are either not one hundred per cent sure you want to do something or your confidence base is very low. What you have to do is look at your motives. Are you doing something because somebody else wants you to, or is it just a flight of fancy? If it's just a dream then it's a natural assumption you're not going to achieve it because your true desire is to not achieve it—after all, if you actually achieved it what would you have to dream about? You have to look at why your negative affirmations are operable. Are they because other people are making your structure or making you structure yourself in a situation you don't really want? Or is it because your confidence base is low?

If you are being negative because of another person then you have to look at what you really want to do; to promote a positive affirmation you have to truly desire the outcome. This is very important.

Positive affirmations work with our attitude towards any situation: I will achieve success in this work goal. I will attain a life structure that makes me happy. I am able to be confident and successful. Caring about oneself is a very positive affirmation that flows over into everything we do: I care about the person I am, I want to be a stronger person, etcetera.

The words 'I want' or 'I should' work potentially in the negative. Instead you need to say, 'I choose to be', or 'I am a more positive person'. 'I am' is one of the most positive focuses possible in an affirmation because what it is saying is that you have, in fact, arrived at a state of success: I am achieving my goal. I am losing weight. I am healthy. I am successful. I care about myself. I love myself. I love others. I feel no fear. I am calm. I am happy. I am successful.

If we write our affirmations on cards and leave them in places where we are going to see them regularly, we are continually affirming the statement. We're putting energy into something that we're creating in our lives. Our mind is like a large computer. It takes on the programming and accepts it regardless of what it is we give ourselves. If we change 'I can't' into 'I am', then our computer changes it. It updates its files. We start to feel more confident. We become more successful. We become more goal-orientated and more centred. By affirming 'I am happy' you actually confront those areas that you are not happy with. You become consciously aware of those situations in your mind and are then in a position to change them, 'I choose to change this situation, I allow myself happiness, I release the fears and restrictions that stop my success and happiness.' You're able to find what is limiting you. You actually change your programming from one in which you are in an uncertain structure because of fears or reservations into one where you are confident because you have looked at your fears and reservations.

You can and should use affirmations every day. From the time you get out of bed in the morning, you decide what you day is going to be like. 'I feel tired!' Waking up that way you are generating an awareness in your programming to stay that way. 'I am exhausted.' What does that say? That you are very tired— your day progresses that way. It doesn't change or gain momentum. So on waking in the morning the first thing you have to do is change whatever you are feeling. If you wake up feeling happy and you actually acknowledge it then that's how the day progresses. Change your negative attitude into a positive one: I feel great. I am happy, I am full of energy, I am ready for the day, nothing is a problem, I can achieve anything, I am able to achieve anything I choose to, I will achieve a successful day at work, I will have a happy day at work, I choose to have a successful day at work.

What we are doing is generating a positive flow of energy from the beginning of our day. It builds momentum as the day progresses. We start to believe and take on more confidence structures as the day progresses, and we end up having a very successful day. Like attracts like. Believe it or not, if you wake up feeling lousy, you have a headache and you feel cranky or disrupted, then you'll tend to create situations in your day that not only reflect this but enhance it as well. You also attract people who are going through similar feelings and emotions. A confident and happy person can change the attitude of a whole office or family structure. By repeating and promoting a confident affirmation about how you feel your confidence will rub off on other people, because it makes them pull themselves out of the rut they've put themselves in. You must have noticed that yourself. When you've been around a happy person you always feel better. When you're around a sad person you always feel more depressed or anxious. By taking the first step to change how you feel, your better feelings will rub off on all the people around you and you will have a successful and fulfilling day.

Affirmations can increase your productivity. They can increase your stamina, they can change the way you see life, create a happier environment to live in and provide a confident direction. You feel more in control of your own power centre. You feel powerful. You become powerful and it effects a positive change in your life. You achieve a lot more in this state than you do when you're feeling depressed and anxious. It affects the health of the body as well. Positive affirmation works on keeping you feeling fit and healthy so you achieve success. You may even exceed your goal and the day becomes more than you actually planned it to be.

Affirmations can change our attitudes. By continually saying them, you de-program the negative data bank, the computer, your mind. It starts to look at the structures that are not effective in your life. The affirmation generates a change in your thinking and opens you to more potential, more direction and allows you the achievement of your goals. You become more successful as an individual, your actions become more confidently based. You create that happy environment for yourself and other people. You may even extend your creativity and expand on what you choose to do. Because you are not limiting what you believe you can or should do, you open up doors that perhaps take you beyond your own expectations.

The steps to affirming are very simple. Write down a list each day. Do your lists say: 'I can't', 'I won't', 'It's impossible'? Turn them into: 'I can', I will' and 'I am' and see the effect for yourself. See how it changes what happens to you.

Write affirmations on cards and have them in your workplace and home to give you an incentive to change your attitude. They work wonderfully well with people who are looking at improving their health, expanding their potential in life, losing weight, doing anything at all. The ultimate rule is that we have to *want* to do something before we can do it. By using affirmations we find out if our desire is really to change something or to leave it as it is. If we realise we really don't want to change something, we can look at the reasons behind it and change that into a situation where we do choose to do it because that's what we really want to do. In other words, we look at where we've set our limitations. The affirmation allows us to look at where we've set limitations that stop us from reaching our true goal. It brings up our subconscious thoughts and makes us deal with them, removing the blocks that stop us achieving and then we go on to be successful.

Fridges, wardrobes, mirrors and walls are all excellent places to place your affirmations. Have a list of them and continuously use them. Do it for a month and take note of the changes. I can guarantee there will be impressive changes.

Affirmations and dreams

The power of dreams is magnified by the thought activity we have during our awakened state. As our days progress and we go through many collective feelings and emotions about the life situations we have to deal with, we are continually working at overcoming the fears and obstacles, the restrictions that life has for us.

Often when I have experienced problems or issues that I found difficult to work through I have found I need to be close to water. I get a lot of answers when I am sitting or meditating close to the water. Just reflecting on anything that may be disturbing me at the time. Through active conscious thought, trying to deal with it through a meditative focus, and using a positive affirmation, I am actually releasing the need to bring out the problem in a subconscious memory or dream state. But nevertheless, whether I have dealt with it successfully, or not at all, I will relive some of the experiences of the day in my sleep state. It will have far less negative impact than it would otherwise since I have basically cleared the issue with a positive affirmation.

The power of affirmations can change the way that we access memory or data of our previous day's experiences. A good example is one I have had myself, where I was pondering on a lot of attitudes and approaches from other people that were disturbing. I found that what I saw while meditating on the water was that the current of the water was moving through the rocks and over the obstacles that were placed before it. There were many leaves and fragments of nature that had fallen in the river and were now creating an obstacle course, yet there were still parts of the river that were crystal clear. The water current moved through every single obstacle, even if it took a lot longer than perhaps the river intended.

It is the same when you are dealing with a problem. It doesn't matter how distressed you feel at the time, you are always going to move through it. With the power of our dreams we are able to bring in an extra, perhaps a bystander's, view from our subconscious level of the effect and influence of whatever we're dealing with. Then through meditation we can help ourselves bring up and look at the situation.

The power of affirmation comes in very handy here. If we can ascertain that we develop or find a fear coming out of a situation we are currently dealing with— perhaps friends want us to go swimming and we are finding it very hard to stay in the water—the fear itself, the recognition of fear, is something that we find very difficult to deal with and we struggle with it.

By meditating we are helping clear out the restrictions that we place on dealing with the fear, the self-imposed reasons that we give ourselves for not dealing with it. Then we are in a position where we can use affirmations to help clear and release the fear, by reaffirming something of a different nature.

In this case look at the water as something very inviting and attractive and look at how you can affirm change in your attitude to the water. Perhaps it's necessary to have swimming lessons and then to work privately on your own, at your own pace, to your own comfort level. By affirming that this is the first step you are taking and actually putting it into some structure, you can change the obstacle. You change the situation so that you are releasing the overall fear; then you are just confronting the reality of that fear, which is really just your inability to swim, not necessarily an independent fear of the water. You can get to the bottom of it!

Now, using the affirmation that you are capable of swimming, your subconscious, while you are sleeping, de-programs all the negative beliefs that you have set up for yourself and then starts allowing you to see the more positive side of yourself.

An affirmation is the formulation of a statement that one wants to make to change a belief pattern. A belief pattern is something that we believe within ourselves. If we believe that we have a toothache that is going to erupt into an infection, we can put enough energy into that to make the infection manifest.

When we look at anything that we do in life we go through periods where we need to work with affirmation to change our programming, or our beliefs, about certain issues, things, situations or circumstances. By affirming something often enough an enpowerment can be created which actually stimulates our belief in something very different; thus we change how we perceive something.

For example, 'I am prosperous.' Now, initially you may say that and find that part of you doesn't believe in it; that part of you will wrestle through from a subconscious level during your dream space, wrestling with your own belief. You get to a point where you believe you should be prosperous and that overpowers your negative belief. The belief will change and suddenly you accept the belief of being prosperous. You may change jobs, you may find that you're attracting more money into your life, you may be prosperous with friendships. It can be a multitude of different circumstances or situations. It is extremely important that when we work with an affirmation we look at the words and what they mean literally and exactly, what they represent and what they are going to influence, direct and attract. We have to be precise about what we are asking ourselves to work with.

When you formulate an affirmation, you must define it specifically. For example, people commonly ask for success but don't find it. They have failed to define 'success'. Does it mean a lot of money, a new house, a new job, a new car, status among peers or within the community? With money, power, status, etcetera, comes responsibility. They are inseparable. You can have anything you want if you are serious about it and have *fully* defined it. What is prosperity? An enormous amount of money? I know a person who only makes $300 per week. He spends $80 for rent and $70 for groceries, he walks to work and banks $600 per month ($7200 per year). This person always has more than he needs and considers himself to be very prosperous. In fact, he's been doing this for some time and has a healthy bank account. He designed his life that way and affirms his prosperity regularly.

A statement like 'I am prosperous' is a very open sort of affirmation. If we are looking at attracting a particular type of prosperity then it is important that we affirm exactly what we want and work with that programming; by going through a very simple process of working with white light, deep breathing and making repeated positive statements to ourselves, aloud and writing them down, over and over again, until the confusion within us ends.

The part of our consciousness that fights against a belief change is what we call the negative ego, which forever works with our negative belief in ourselves. When a negative belief structure is operable, it is like a small child. It keeps nagging at us and telling us that something is impossible; it can so tire us and weaken our resistance that we give in and accept what it is saying to us.

If we defend ourselves a little more and we just say, 'No, I'm not giving in. This is the way it is and I will not accept less. I am succeeding. I am attracting this and I am having this happen', then the outcome is that we override the negative belief pattern and the positive belief pattern takes over. We succeed with our positive affirmation. Again, the affirmation must be totally positive.

This can work with dreams. If we have a recurring dream and are finding it very difficult to deal with or to work out what it is trying to tell us or help us with, we can actually affirm that we recognise that we are in the midst of a dream pattern that is very difficult to interpret and we would like to have clarity. We affirm that we are able to understand and relate to what the dream is telling us. By saying it over and again and going through the affirmation process before we go to sleep at night, during our sleep we can actually stimulate the attraction of success of that affirmation and unravel the confusion of the dream. This stops the confusing dream state from occurring repeatedly.

One of the most important elements of a successful affirmation is that it is repeated on a regular basis. You can say it out loud, within your mind, write it down, record it. The most important thing is that you are continually absorbing it to help you de-program the negative ego and accept it as conscious fact. This in itself helps us make a total change in what we allow ourselves to attract in our lives and in our future.

The more simplistic the affirmation the easier it is for the mind to digest. Let's do a list of very simple, basic affirmations and what they mean.

I am successful—means that you are achieving success (don't forget to define exactly what success means to you).

I personally empower myself—means that you allow yourself to be all powerful.

I am successful in love—that is a statement of fact. You are making a statement that you are successful in romance.

I allow myself happiness—means that you release all fears and restrictions that you have about achieving this goal.

I accept change in my life—means that you are not as rigid with your beliefs or views.

Stuart Wilde wrote one of the most powerful affirmations I ever heard and it remains my favourite today, although I've added the second half of each line for my own clarification.[6]

I am infinite—I have no beginning. I have no end.
I am eternal—I have always been and I always will be.
I am immortal—I have always lived and I always will live.
I am universal—I am all things.

We can work with affirmations in our dreams by affirming when we wake in the morning that our desire is to understand what the dream is all about. We are encouraging our subconscious to slowly integrate our awareness, and that may happen as the day goes on. Like a clock filled with information, as we tick along we pick up particle after particle of information and data, until finally we put the complexity of the whole thing into a format that we understand. Suddenly the penny drops and we recognise what the dream was all about. The affirmation has allowed you to achieve that. By reaffirming before we go to bed our desire to understand our dreams we are activating a subconscious programming to achieve our goal.

It may not happen on the first night. You may have to go through a period

[6]Stuart Wilde, *Affirmations*, 1987, White Dove International: Taos, New Mexico

of time where you are just working with the affirmation. The main thing is that you don't give up and you don't get disappointed and you don't allow that negative ego to come and attack this wonderful line of communication that's opening up in your subconscious. Instead, give it time and allow it to release and open up the door of knowledge and understanding that you are seeking. As the day progresses you will find that it unfolds, expands, and slowly you are integrating an awareness and understanding of what your symbolism represents. As I said with the sequence dream, affirming that we want to understand it brings clarity and understanding.

To deal with an abstract dream, affirm on awakening: 'I now choose to understand what each symbol represents in my dream.' Then mentally think of all the symbols, affirming that you allow yourself to understand in your conscious state. 'I allow myself in my conscious state to understand what this symbol means.' Allow each symbol to flow through and say the same affirmation before each one, that you are allowing yourself to understand what the symbols represent.

If you are confronted by a dream that causes you to wake up frightened, say: 'I affirm and accept acknowledgment of what my fear is. I now choose to understand it and allow myself the understanding during my awakened state.' This means that you are allowing yourself to slowly integrate the awareness of what your fear is and deal with it.

If a dream has caused you to wake up confused, affirm: 'I now accept and affirm the clarity of understanding and I release my confusion totally from my thought pattern and accept knowledge and clarity.'

What's important with affirmations is that you allow yourself to feel that what you're saying is very real. If you are just parroting off a phrase it will have no effect or influence on you at all. If you are really putting momentum into what you are saying and you allow yourself to have a fight with your negative ego, which is trying to dismiss what you are trying to create, then what you find is your programming will change. Slowly you will start to integrate and accept the new programming.

APPENDIX A

Meditation Made Easy

I've added this section to explain meditation and how it relates to dreams as well as to present specific meditations to assist you in understanding your dreams. (See the section in Chapter 5 on Self-help Techniques, pages 90–94.)

I've taught meditation for over fourteen years and I still see many people who misunderstand the purpose, the end result, and how it is actually accomplished. Though there are hundreds of books on the subject, few actually detail specific techniques that can be used by the lay person on a daily basis. However, almost everyone has done meditation at one time or another without realising it. Simple daydreams become a form of meditation; they occur when you direct your attention to a specific subject, deliberately excluding all other thought from your mind. Prayer can also be a form of meditation.

Meditation is used daily by millions of people. It may be used to keep you centred, earthed or grounded, and balanced, as well as providing a means to reduce stress. It increases your awareness and gives you clarity and direction when important decisions are to be made.

Meditation is no longer a secret mind technique used exclusively by High Lamas and Yogis to achieve enlightenment, nor do you have to join some esoteric religious cult to learn it. It is used daily by high-level business executives, secretaries, bus drivers, chefs and pilots, all very normal people in normal daily circumstances just like you.

Stop and focus on your thought patterns for a moment. You think about having a bite to eat, then switch to a few delicious moments on a secluded beach with that favourite someone in your life, then the weather catches your attention and you ponder the rain and how long it will last, or the sunshine and how long that will last before it rains, then your finances offer some interesting mental gymnastics that are usually depressing so you wander back to the fantasy with your favourite person until you realise that can't become a reality because your finances won't allow too much extravagance so you might just as well focus on the task at hand which is getting ready for work and that means selecting something with a colour which is reflective of the mood you're now in, et cetera, ad infinitum.

Your mind functions much like a ship without a captain. Each member of the crew gets to drive for a while until they get bored and the next takes a turn. There is no direction, no particular destination at which to arrive so the pattern of the course is very random.

Most of us tend to live our lives the same way. As thoughts arrive we react accordingly, with only very short-term goals, like getting that snack, deliberately going to the petrol station to refuel our vehicle, or just getting dressed in the morning.

Meditation done regularly allows us to regain some degree of control over the direction of our minds. Just as with riding an exercise bike, we don't gain instant fitness or see any immediate improvement in our physique, but used regularly we gradually gain control over the shape of our body, so it is with meditation.

The thought sequence above is quite typical and deserves more attention. Looking at it a bit more carefully, we see that the majority of thoughts reflect either the past or future activities. Ask yourself, 'Why is my body living in the now while my brain is continually living in the past or future?'

We also see something else which has crept into our thoughts—worry. Our current finances are a source of worry and mind occupation; because that concern has been raised, finances may very well come up in our dream patterns but presented as a different symbol. Seeing the situation presented in a different way may very well allow us to see a solution to the problem.

You will not see instant answers during meditation, nor will solutions become apparent immediately afterward, usually because your expectations get in the way. You must learn to let things happen in their own good time and trust that 'the highest good' will prevail. Like using the exercise bike, in time your awareness will become finely tuned and your intuition will guide you unerringly.

The role of meditation in this case is to provide a vehicle which allows the conscious mind to view a subconscious solution that is not clouded by symbols or other confusing thoughts not relevant to the problem. And how does that happen? The non-meditating person has thought patterns similar to those mentioned above with few of the thoughts ever thought through to completion— thus, they reappear in the dream state. A typical example would be feeling stuck in your job and wanting to get out of it to obtain one on a managerial level so you can have more privileges, money, prestige, power, whatever. You may even have a moment of daydreaming and visualising what it *would* feel like if you had that position. At night you might have a dream in which you find yourself on a journey which leads you to the bank of a muddy river you are not able to cross. On the other side you can see green grassy slopes bathed in sunshine and tranquility. And then you awaken. The next night you dream of sitting down to a huge banquet but to your surprise you have no hands with which to eat, so you sit there just looking at the food in frustration.

Both of these dreams represent a problem of accomplishment with no apparent solution. The first dream is pretty straightforward but the second is a bit more bizarre. Subsequent dreams may even be nightmarish as you become more frustrated with finding a solution to your problem.

Meditation conditions the mind so that you are able to clear away the flak and focus directly on a problem by defining its parameters very concisely. You give the problem to the Universe and forget it. Usually within a day or two, as your mind is aimlessly wandering through its daily random pattern, a light bulb turns on; you may see yourself taking a night course which will give you the necessary skills and realise that some manager is about to quit or that the company is looking for someone for a position they haven't been able to fill. The bridge appears over the muddy water and you are able to accomplish your goal.

While you are learning to meditate you should not take issues into the meditation. That may come at a later time. Just relax, clear your mind, and focus so that you are able to put things into perspective. Then, after your meditation, you can look at the problem with a very clear head. You should also try to let go of expectations as that is the greatest source of self-defeat there is. In other words, if you do happen to be wrestling with a problem, don't go into a meditation and come out saying, 'OK, where's the answer?' I guarantee you just won't have one. You should simply train your mind for single-mindedness of thought using one of the meditation techniques I have detailed (p.90–94), or another one you particularly like which you may already know of.

Whichever technique you choose, stay with it and don't experiment with a different one until you achieve some degree of success with the one you used first. What constitutes success here?

1. Being able to stay focused on a single subject for more than about one minute at a time.

2. Being comfortable with staying in a meditation for a longer period than usual (that is, without becoming fidgety).

3. Being able to bring yourself back to the subject when your mind does wander without undue stress about it.

4. Finding your sleep is more restful.

5. A feeling of clarity in your thought patterns immediately afterward.

6. A supreme feeling of peace and calm following the meditation.

People who meditate frequently will also find an increase in dream activity. Not all dreams are centred around daily life problems. You may discover you are not only more aware of dreams involving astral travel but that you are doing more of it.

Guidelines for meditation

What is a meditation?
How do I start?
Where should I be?
How should I sit?
Should I close my eyes?
What if I fall asleep?
When should I meditate?
What should I meditate on?
How long should a meditation last?
What should my feelings reflect?
What if my mind wanders off on another subject?

I think these questions are fairly representative of the ones I am asked and the ones I sought answers to when I began meditating. Let's just take them one at a time so you can begin your meditation with less anxiety than most people, who wonder what is going to happen, when it is going to happen, and how intense it will be.

What is a meditation?

A thesaurus might say prayer, cogitation, contemplation, study, deliberation, reflection, speculation, analysis, thinking. Meditation is all of those things. Most of all, however, it is a time to train and gently coax your mind into a single thought pattern which you are able to control at any time you choose to do so and for as long as you choose.

The practicality of this is that you can focus your attention on a single project without the interruptions normally associated with various thought processes. Using regular meditation, your daily work routine becomes much more efficient timewise and your ability to reason becomes much more focused.

How do I start?

Meditation is a spiritual experience and you are therefore opening yourself up to the spirit realm. It is best to always begin with a short prayer asking for the protection of The Light from any dark or mischievous entities: for guidance, wisdom and teaching; and to bring forward that which is for 'the highest good'.

Just as you 'open up' with a prayer at the beginning of your meditation you should 'close down' at the conclusion. There are two ways of doing this. The first is to visualise golden hoops spinning down around you from above; the second method is to visualise yourself being sealed in a cocoon of white light or a bubble of golden light. Closing down is very important so that you don't leave yourself open to collecting the dirty laundry being mentally carried around and projected by people nearby.

Where should I be?

Quite simply, the general rule is that you will want to be in a quiet place where you will not be disturbed by telephones, television or other people barging in on you. Many people like the bathroom or toilet because they are not likely to be disturbed and they are usually fairly quiet places, especially late in the evening just before bed. One of my favourite places is the bathtub. Light a single candle, turn the lights out—you might put some scented oil in the bathwater and/or light some incense—fill the tub as full as you can and completely submerge yourself without overflowing the water onto the floor. The hotter the water the better. I'll get into this one in more detail later in the section on candle meditations (page 115).

How should I sit?

This question has been the subject of some controversy. A purist might have you use nothing but a full or half lotus position, sitting with your back straight,

Full lotus position

Half lotus position

hands on knees, palms up with thumb and forefinger of each hand forming an O with middle, ring and little fingers extended. A full lotus is nearly impossible for a beginner but a half lotus while sitting on a pillow isn't bad and may quickly become quite comfortable. You may just rest your hands in your lap, one on top of the other, palms up. You may also use a chair in which you can sit up straight without your back touching. Some people prefer to lie down but I find this position much too conducive to falling asleep.

Basically speaking, you should get comfortable but not so much so that you nod off when you relax.

Should I close my eyes?

This all depends on the type of meditation you are doing. If you are using a candle as the focus of your thoughts or are watching the aura of an object (I discuss auras later, on page 115), you will not want to close your eyes. Most other meditations will come together for you more readily if you do close your eyes.

What if I fall asleep?

Remember that one of the goals of meditation is relaxation. If you do fall asleep it usually means that you are too comfortable when you relax, that is, you are lying down, or sitting back in a very comfortable chair. It can also mean that it is either very early in the morning or very late at night when you are most likely sleepy to begin with. I've experienced some very nice meditation sessions both lying down and in my papa-san chair, but I've been relatively alert at the time.

When should I meditate?

A meditation early in the morning can be a great way to start the day and a meditation in the evening is a good way to make the transition from the busy day to a restful evening. I generally prefer the evening meditation as a nice transition to the peace and tranquility I seek prior to retiring for the evening. I am also partial to candle meditations which work better in the darkness and calm of evening. Between 7 and 9 in the evening it is usually dark and calm, and I am not yet tired enough to go to sleep.

I know some people who like to go for a walk in a nearby park during their lunch break. A short meditation here can be a great mid-day break.

What should I meditate on?

This again depends on the type of meditation you are doing. Remember that the object of the exercise is to keep your mind focused on a single thought train, regardless of the subject matter. As I mentioned earlier, you need to pick a meditation with a subject, objective and technique you can get comfortable with for more than thirty seconds and for more than one session.

How long should a meditation last?

The duration of any single meditation depends entirely on the individual and how comfortable you are with that subject and technique. A minimum time to get anything out of the exercise would be five to ten minutes for the first few tries. After that you should try to extend your time in the same way an athlete tries for increased distance and time. I've had very successful meditations lasting about seven minutes, but on the other hand two hours is not uncommon for me. I have gone as long as four hours with a meditation I just really enjoyed and didn't want to quit. During classes I do guided group meditations which average fifteen to twenty minutes, and everyone seems to be very comfortable with that time frame.

What should my feelings reflect?

Probably one of the most misunderstood areas of meditation and the largest stumbling block to enlightenment is an attempt at precognition of a particular outcome. *Just relax into whatever happens.* If you don't understand the symbols you see, you may ask for assistance from your teacher, a more experienced practitioner, or your spirit guide. (More on high self and the spirit guides on pages 10–13.)

What if my mind wanders off on another subject?

Even experienced practitioners find this happening and it is something you can't really prevent. You will find that some times are better than others for retaining your focus. Occasionally it is very difficult to keep out the flood of outside thoughts and you feel like throwing in the towel and just forgetting the whole exercise. Don't quit; this is quite a normal experience and is accounted for by an overactive left brain that is afraid it is being left out of something. Left brain is the one that always wants to argue, question all incoming data, worry about trivial daily activities, and is the source of most of the negativity you feel toward others.

The solution is to treat your mind as you would a small child you have taken for a walk. You don't slam them back on the path, you gently coax them to return to the journey you've chosen: 'I see we've got a little off the path here so let's just return where we left off and see how much farther we can go this time.'

Specific meditations

If you've never meditated before, a guided meditation is often the best way to begin. Obviously it would be quite difficult to read a meditation and try to do it at the same time. Although you could have someone else read it to you, the best way to do it is by reading the script yourself into a small tape recorder. You will benefit much more from this because you are listening to your own voice guide you into the meditation. Add five to fifteen minutes of soft music, then bring yourself out using the script provided.

Bringing back past memory

Many dreams are difficult to interpret because our mind presents those unsolved daily life problems to us using symbols in an effort to allow us a different perspective on the problem. Those symbols are not necessarily the same for all people so it is important that each person unlock their own personal symbology.

The purpose of this meditation is to bring up symbolism that can reactivate your conscious awareness of what you are storing deep in the subconscious. The symbolism will then, over a period of days or weeks, turn into a more simplistic and understandable dream that you will be able to make sense of. You can also record this symbolism and try and work out what each symbol represents to you. By doing this you may also get an insight into what you have collected and stored in your deep subconscious memory. We tend to store a lot of memory on a day-to-day basis that we don't consciously think about and within this storage will be a collection of unresolved issues—emotions over situations which have caused us anger and frustration, or where we have had our feelings hurt by someone, guilt and remorse. We store this collectively in our deep subconscious (solar plexus chakra) and over a period of time find it hard to re-access and/or understand. Nevertheless, when our day is stressful or we undergo similar emotions, we will re-activate the feelings from the past in their confusing state during our dreaming. This meditation is designed to clear out confusion and bring back clarity not only to help with past traumas but to stop new or current issues from being stored without resolution.

Begin Take a deep breath, in through your nose ... hold it ... now release this breath slowly ... out through your mouth ... and with this breath slowly expel all the tensions held within your body.

Take another deep breath ... hold it ... again release this breath slowly, and with it let go of any worries or cares held within your body. Now you are completely relaxed.

Visualise a vibrant ray of white light covering you and entering your body from above (like standing on stage with a spotlight shining down from above you), filling you and massaging through your entire body. Allow the energy of this light to massage and flow through every part of your being. Feel yourself gently releasing all the concerns of your physical and mental self—completely relax.

Feel a bubble of white energy form around you. Inside the bubble feel yourself as you are now. You are beginning a journey down into the retrieval of your memory.

You are going to open up all files that exist at a very deep level, right back to birth. You are opening a door all the way back to birth.

You are going to relate to being in the bubble at the age you are now. You feel who you are, this day, today and how it feels to be cocooned in this lovely vibration of white energy. Relaxing with this foetal position as an adult, cocooned and protected from everything. Nothing is negative, you are in a totally positive frame of mind. Focus love and a feeling of love within the bubble so that you feel in harmony with yourself and with the world.

Just relax and get into that harmonious feeling and balance. Now accept that you wish to accelerate your memory backward to the point of birth. Feel the momentum inside the bubble, focusing back in time until you can feel yourself becoming a tiny little child, very small. You are not vulnerable but totally protected in this white cocoon. Just like being inside the mother's womb, totally protected and guided into expansion and birth.

Feel a vibration of gold light around you, drawing its influence into the cocoon and tapping into your cellular memory. I want you to say to yourself, 'It is my free will to release and open my memory of all life experience that I have restricted and filed at a dormant level in my subconscious level.' Just relax with this and allow it to focus. Feel the gold light moving through you and helping you open up your files.

Feel a window inside you opening up, fresh air expanding and opening and breathing in an awareness. All the memory and stored files that exist there. Lots of different symbols are opening up to you. Feel them opening up into your subconscious mind. Register a memory of these symbols.

(Note that you may see a collection of abstract shapes and forms such as animals, jewellery, geometric figures, colours, et cetera, and also a collection of feelings and emotions. Do not try to use the six symbols given later as they serve a different purpose. Relax and let your own symbols present themselves to you, don't try to create them.)

You slowly bring up one symbol at a time and ask what that symbol means. It can be a word or it can be a feeling. Initially that is fine and all you need to work with. It will expand naturally as your memory returns and you open to the reality of that feeling or sensation.

Feel a silver ray rising from deep in the ground, coming up through each chakra centre in the body. It rises through the crown chakra and gently cascades down around the body. Repeat, 'I acknowledge and expand and open every file within my subconscious.' You will make this affirmation through each chakra centre all the way up.

Relax and enjoy your symbols now as you listen to the music and mentally review each symbol as it passes before you so you can record them later.

[Place five to fifteen minutes of music here.]

Now it is time to return. Focus your consciousness back into your physical body, centre yourself by wiggling your toes and flexing your body slightly ... take a deep breath ... when you are ready, open your eyes and relax.

Write down what you received as symbols. Record your feelings and impressions about each symbol. For example, 'WHITE DOG—felt anger and anxiety, possibly reflecting the frustration over my noisy neighbour when I try to sleep in on the weekend and he is mowing the lawn at 7.30 am.'

Using symbols to unlock memory

Mini focus

Using symbols in the way I am about to describe is designed to help you unravel your current and future dreams before they go into such complex symbolism they become difficult to understand. You are going to be given a symbol which will be your key to unlock future storage.

There are six symbols:

a silver disc

a golden star

a pink rose

a clear quartz crystal

a pyramid

a red heart

You will be taken through a focus where you are asked to choose one of these symbols as your key.

Begin Relax ... take a nice deep breath. Clear your mind.

I want you to visualise a ray of violet light coming from above you and washing through every part of your being. Feel it going through all centres in your body and feel your centres opening as your focus then returns. Feel your base chakra breathing, opening, opening and expanding as you inhale. Move up to your spleen chakra—feel it breathe, opening and expanding as you inhale. Now move up to your solar plexus chakra, feel it breathe, feel it opening and expanding; now move up to your heart chakra, feel it breathe, as you breathe in feel it opening and expanding. Now move up to your throat chakra—as you breathe in feel it opening and expanding, now move up to your brow chakra and as you breathe in feel it opening and expanding ... Now move up to your crown chakra, feel it breathe, as you breathe in feel it opening and expanding and as you do a trapdoor opens.

The trapdoor opens and now reveals in front of you a closed box. In the box is a symbol. Look at the list of key symbols above—you will feel drawn to the symbol that is yours, and the box will open automatically and present you with your key symbol.

I want you to reach out and accept the symbol and then say to yourself, 'I now affirm this is the symbol that I will use to expand and open up my dormant files. It now becomes my key to retrieve memory and open it up to my conscious level of awareness so that I can deal with it in a conscious state or in a subconscious state of dreaming.'

[*Insert music here if you wish to extend this meditation or you may come out as below.*]

When you are ready, it is time to return. Slowly take a nice deep breath. Slowly re-focus on your physical body . . . open your eyes . . . and relax.

The candle

Fire is an extremely powerful element and a flame meditation is an extension of that power. I particularly like candle flames for meditation for a variety of reasons. They are enjoyable, easy to use and readily available. They also provide a great vehicle for instant and visible success which is a tremendous confidence-builder.

A candle flame is an especially good object to use for meditation because it is easy to enjoy, it provides for tremendous emotional release in that it is very calming and has so many aspects to the flame itself. For example, you can really appreciate the wonder and beauty of the natural gifts of light and heat which come in fairly large quantity from a small, simple candle flame. That can be a meditation in and of itself. Let's look at some of the many ways of using a candle for meditation, beginning with the aura of the flame.

The aura

The existence of auras has been seen and proven beyond doubt by means of Kirlian photography. It has also been shown, through Kirlian photography, that even if a leaf is torn or cut in half, the aura still defines the entire leaf. Amputees have described itching, pain and other sensations in missing limbs. A Kirlian photograph would show the existence of an aura which describes the entire limb.

The aura does not give life to inanimate matter like a candle, but rather is a reflection of the energy given off by anything inanimate. All living things produce an auric field, and all inanimate objects absorb or collect particles of energy from animate structures, so we can perceive an aura around all things.

Even candle flames have auras and they are particularly easy to see. Begin by noticing the various parts of the flame, beginning with the wick itself. Then, notice the very small, seemingly empty, air space between the wick and the blue area at the base of the flame, said to be the hottest area. Just above the wick is a shadowed area which I call the Madonna of the Flame. I always feel an emanation of tremendous power from this area. From the base of the flame up through the Madonna, the flame is very thin and transparent. However, as we move into the orange area of the flame, we see that it is very dense and not transparent at all. The very tip of the flame is a fascinating area in that it is a uniquely feathered blending of the orange area gradually fading into the air above it. The sides of a calm flame usually appear crisp and clear as though they had been defined by a razor's edge.

In a darkened room, there is a distinct glow immediately around the flame itself. While the flame is elliptical, the glow is perfectly round. The best definition of this aura can be seen if you know how to let your eyes go into soft focus or by focusing on a point just above the flame and across the room. Soft focus is the state you are in when you are looking directly at something but daydreaming about something else which is actually holding your attention. It takes a bit of practice but that is the best technique for seeing auras in anything. With your eyes in soft focus you may well see a rainbow of colour dancing within this aura or energy field. You may or may not also experience seeing a fire deva. (A deva is a lower angelic spirit form which controls the elements: fire, water, earth, wind, wood. The Hawaiians call them *menehune*, which means little people or nature spirits.)

Mirror of the mind

A candle flame is also a wonderful mirror of the mind as it is sensitive to both air currents and brain waves. Yes, I said brain waves. Just find a room with doors and windows shut so that no air currents affect the flame. Turn out all light except a single candle flame. Put the candle in the centre of the floor and sit on the floor facing it (I like a half lotus position but you may use any one you find comfortable) but some distance away (1.5–2 metres/4–6 feet). You may also place it at the centre of a table while you sit upright in a chair with feet flat on the floor and your hands resting on top of your thighs with palms up. Take a few meditative breaths to calm your mind and body. Look into the flame while emptying your mind of all thoughts and just enjoy the being of the flame itself. If your mind is calm, the flame will be calm. If your mind is racing with thoughts and frustrations the flame will mirror it precisely. The objective is to use the *unlimited power of your mind* to firstly still the candle flame, and secondly see how tall you can make it reach. This is not only a very calming exercise, it is also a basic technique for training yourself in the art of telekinesis (causing physical objects to move with mind power alone). This is a great confidence-builder and demonstration of the reality of telekinesis which can be performed successfully by a first-time student. It is also one of my husband's favourite meditations. He does it frequently.

Golden threads

As you look into the flame of the candle, slowly begin closing your eyes; before they are shut you will see strands of gold reaching out from the flame. You can make them longer or shorter by adjusting the tilt of your head and/or the degree your eyes are actually open. The objective is to connect yourself to the flame by these golden threads and feel the energy flow into you from the flame.

Using a mantra

A mantra is simply a word or group of words being repeated like a chant for the duration of the meditation. The purpose is to invoke a spiritual essence. Some commercial meditation groups like Transcendental Meditation (TM) give each of their clients a personal secret mantra which they cannot divulge to anyone. Because modern Western meditation stems from origins in India, most mantras currently in use consist of Indian words. However, short prayers, verses from prayers, biblical passages, or any other group of words or numbers may be used. The object is to get them into a rhythm as they are repeated so that you can achieve a oneness with the sound. The mantra or chant does not have to be spoken aloud, being just as effective if vocalised internally. The exact origin of chanting may never be known as various primitive cultures all over the world have used it for thousands of years in association with witchcraft, healing, invoking spirits and meditation. It is interesting that 'civilised' cultures speak of older cultures in which the people lived very close to the earth as 'primitive', and yet that is precisely the focus (living close to the earth) of many people of 'modern' outlook. Using a mantra is very much like riding an exercise bike. It is either a lot of work for no immediate or apparent gain, or else you will rapidly find yourself in a trance-like state, mechanically saying the same words over and over. There is no instant gratification but the work does produce excellent results over the long haul in terms of your ability to achieve single-mindedness.

Common mantras include 'Om mani padmi om', 'Om namo bagavaté vasu de via', 'Hari Krishna, Hari Hari, Hari Krishna', 'Hail Mary, full of grace...', '1-2-3-4'.

With incense

For variation and an increase in mental sensitivity, place a stick of burning incense in front of your candle. Remember what I said about the flame being a mirror of your mind and how sensitive the flame is to your thoughts? The smoke is even more sensitive to your thought waves. If you happen to have two people meditating together you will frequently see two plumes of smoke rising and reacting separately to the thoughts of the two people. See if you can pick out which plume is relating to you and which one to your partner. It's fun, it's informative, and it is instant feedback on the state of your mind. Just as the candle flame reflects the calmness of your mind so does the column of smoke. The object is to see how high you can make it climb without being swirled or dissipated. This meditation is also conducive to becoming one with the smoke as it curls and rises. You will find yourself very calm and relaxed afterward.

Guided group meditations

I use guided meditations for working with groups as it tends to focus the energy of the group, making the energy of the group more powerful. It also helps to weld the group so they are working together rather than as individuals.

What I call guided meditation some other people call creative visualisation. It is where someone takes you through a meditation providing the scenery for you; for example, I may play some very soft music and describe a beautiful sunset and ask the group to visualise themselves walking along a beach watching the sunset. This is a wonderful way of helping the individuals in the group to increase their power of concentration. I have guided meditation tapes available for those who prefer that type of meditation as it can be done individually as well as in a group situation.

Begin   I want you to take a nice deep breath, in through your nose and out through your mouth.

Just relax...

I want you to visualise a vibrant ray of white light pouring down from the Creator, over your body, feel it washing not only over your body but right through every part of your being, like gentle raindrops penetrating through every part of your being.

Feel the white light gently massaging and relaxing you, every part of you.

Take a nice deep breath through your nose, hold on to it, and as you exhale out through your mouth say to yourself, relax, relax.

Relax and let go of all tension and stress, feel your body relaxing as you breathe deeply in through your nose and out through your mouth, feel your mind relaxing as you breathe in deeply and slowly exhale.

I want you to clear your mind of all thoughts, take three deep breaths in through your nose and out through your mouth ... Relax ... let go of all thought ...

I now want you to see yourself wrapped in a vibrant ray of white light. Feel yourself now totally relaxed as this white light forms a cloud-like shape all around you and then expands in your awareness as it grows in dimension, glowing vibrantly all around you, just relax and enjoy the nurturing taking place in your cloud-like environment.

In your mind's eye I want you to visualise a rose, a very vibrant lush pink rose, see the colour, feel the presence of this rose in front of you ... now see the rose changing in colour, from a soft gentle pink to a darker shade, a vibrant red, feeling the colour reaching out toward you and opening up your emotions, as the rose opens to you you open to the rose, feel your heart centre now opening up and pouring out love toward the rose, feel this love being absorbed by the rose and a feeling of love being sent back toward you, take a deep breath, and as you exhale feel yourself absorbing the love returned to you from the rose ...

As you relate to this wonderful feeling of love being reflected from the rose to you and back to the rose again become aware of something opening up inside of you, and a feeling of release, of freedom without emotional or mental restrictions coming over you, you are now spiritually and physically free of all restrictions, relax and bask in this beautiful feeling, let it overwhelm you ...

Use all your senses to feel and relate to the outpouring of love from this rose and as you do become more in tune with the rose, feel the colour change now ... not only a red but a vibrant rainbow of light connecting at your heart centre and extending itself down to your base centre, feel the love now opening up all your centres, starting at the base centre, feel the love pouring in and all restrictions being released as it rises up to your spleen, solar plexus, heart centre, throat centre, brow centre, and crown centre ...

Feel the rainbow opening up an empathy to all around you, once again, relax and bask in this feeling ...

Now you are a spectrum of colour, a rainbow ... feel this rainbow penetrating through every part of your being, pulsating, glowing in love and peace, feel in harmony with yourself and all around you.

I want you now to focus once again on the vibrant red rose, open to the love connecting you to it and feel a feeling of unconditional love between you and the rose ... and now the rose is turning into a vibrant glow of pink light, feel it envelop you and you in turn becoming a vibrant pink glow of energy and light, take a deep breath and drink in the magnificence of your own being, and now feel yourself filled with unconditional love; allow yourself to float in this feeling of love and feel yourself opening up and being nurtured, growing in awareness of yourself in tune with the love all around you ... relax and float freely.

I will leave you here for a few moments to explore your feelings and emotions and when it is time to return I will call you back ... just relax ...

When you're ready it is time to return, feel yourself in attunement with yourself and with everyone else in the room ... take a deep breath and slowly focus on your body ... when you are ready open your eyes and relax.

APPENDIX B

Crystals

Crystals are very powerful tools to use during meditation or our sleep state because they can enhance the clarity of the meditation or dream, adding energy as well as giving you protection from negative influences. Different types of crystals can be programmed to work with healing the body, balancing out our mental anguish or thought pattern to regenerate our physical energy and vitality.

Crystals have an energy field of their own and we can program them to assist us with concentration, health improvement, life balance and harmony, creating prosperity and happiness, achieving good sleep, to wake refreshed and revitalised.

Programming a crystal

The easiest way to program a crystal is to sit calmly and clear the mind of all thought. Play some music to soothe and relax you. Ask yourself what you want the crystal to be programmed for, write it down and look at it to make sure you have the complete detail of what you want. Then hold your crystal, focus a feeling of love through your hands into it. Then slowly program the crystal with the idea of what you would like it to assist you with.

Crystals are the perfectly geometric matter of nature. Through a combination of forces—water, heat and pressure—elements are transformed, their tiny particles forming a structure that focuses, transforms and amplifies energy. They affect both physical and mental energy and as such are especially useful in healing.

Sometimes we see what we call 'phantom structures' in a crystal. This is a crystal inside a crystal which gives the appearance of little mountains forming inside the main crystal. Phantom structures amplify the potency of the crystal. If we are using a crystal for focus then one with a phantom structure would help us with clarity, adding a greater dimension to that clarity. Occasionally we see in a crystal something called a window, a box-like structure normally at the point of the crystal. It is in fact a tiny square or cube-like inclusion. The window in a crystal is the same as a door in your house. It expands your awareness or potential awareness with anything you are meditating on. It would be very valuable to use a crystal with a window for meditation because it would expand the potential you see in your meditation.

We sometimes see rainbow structures in a crystal. A rainbow signifies good fortune or good luck.

Green 'moss' growing within signifies money and attracts prosperity or financial gain.

A clear quartz crystal, if totally clear, is called a male crystal. If it has a cloud-like formation within it then it has a feminine energy as well. You can have a mixture of both in the one crystal, giving the balance of yin and yang.

Clear quartz crystals are wonderful for meditating. You can program the crystal just by focusing pure love into it and then telling it what you'd like it to do. You might program it to create balance and harmony in your home environment, help you with study, anything at all.

There are many different ways of cleaning crystals. I prefer the simplest method, focusing love through the crystal, blowing it through with a deep breath and then rubbing it with rose oil. When you decide to re-program your crystal, just focus love within the crystal and then mentally state your intention: 'I now choose to release the programming in the crystal and open the crystal to new programming.' Then extend your thinking to what you'd like to program it with once again.

The energy and general use of crystals

The environment we live in and everything in it has an effect on us, due to the energy of living matter. For example, when it is a lovely hot sunny day and we sit outside and bask in it we enjoy the energy from the sun which gives us vitality and warmth; when we go for a swim in the sea we appreciate the way the water relaxes us and we savour this special time; when we potter about in the garden we feel the energy of the plants, we enjoy working with nature and watching the growth of the plants we tend. Crystals are living energy fields of their very own. They emit a vital current or flow of energy and we as human beings relate to it. For some it is a conscious recognition but for most it is at a subconscious level.

Adventurine   Works on general healing of the physical body. It also works on clearing out traumas and restrictions.

Agate   Normally in a plate form. Like amethyst it is very good for cleansing or resting other crystals on.

Alexandrite   Works on balancing the mind and emotions to reveal one's own wisdom as well as working very well with the circulatory system. Also works to calm and rebalance animals in times of stress.

Amber   A very beautiful honey-gold crystal that is actually a tree resin. Amber works with increasing and generating our energy.

Amethyst   Works on cleansing the aura; if we have it around our home it keeps the energy clear. Resting other crystals on an amethyst geode overnight cleanses and clears them.

Aquamarine   Works with the reproductive system, stabilising and balancing the uterine area in a woman.

Azurite   Maintains harmony and stability with relationships; generally assists with communication and allows self expression.

Bloodstone   Works with cleansing the blood and revitalising the system, replenishing oxygen or oxygenation of the blood.

Calcite   Allows us to be in touch with the honesty of our feelings; clarity and motivation with self awareness.

Carnelian   Works very well on the respiratory tract and the blood supply, cleansing and purifying the filtration system of the body.

Chrysocolla   Helps us work with inner peace, being in touch with oneself and all around us, inner happiness and tranquillity.

Chrysoprase   Excellent for assisting us to be in touch with our more creative side, adventurous, excellent to work with clearing fears and restrictions in our belief structure.

Citrine   Excellent for sufferers of arthritis, sprains or strains as it assists in relieving inflammation; also good for digestion.

Clear quartz If we wear the quartz crystal close to the body it will amplify the way we feel. If we are happy it will radiate that happiness, if we are in pain, it will exaggerate our feeling of the pain. If in our environment, this crystal can be programmed to work with assisting us in life generally, and will assist us with clarity and absorption of information.

Diamond The clearest of all stones and its potency is far greater even than that of the clear quartz crystal. It works very well for focus and direction.

Emerald Works on emotional stability, physical energy and stabilising our health structure.

Fluorite Excellent in a crystal layout over the body to bring back balance to the physical/etheric levels of our being. It will assist us with maintaining the thoughts we are working on, keeping us on track; excellent to have close to us while studying or in a position where we need our memory. Used with meditation it can assist us with aligning with our guidance or higher self and relaxing and focusing in meditation.

Garnet A very grounding stone. It is a very caring and loving stone that works on balancing our energy.

Jade Will maintain balance in the uterine area, excellent for fertility of body as well as opening up creativity in the mind; it is also excellent to wear when one requires confidence and self esteem.

Kunzite Will promote one's awareness of inner strength, wisdom; helps stabilise our thought pattern when we are confused or unwell; it will assist in rebalancing.

Lapis lazuli What we call the 'deep inner sanctuary'. It works with giving inner courage and strength for emotional crises.

Malachite Releases life restrictions and assists with opening up one's life path, prosperity and happiness.

Moldavite Aligns us with our spiritual purpose and life path, motivates spiritual awareness.

Moonstone Provides a wonderful focus for meditation and general harmony in life. Moonstone works very well with the reproductive system of a woman's body.

Peridot   Releases negative programming, whether self-created or the influence of a negative nature in our environment.

Pyrite   Assists us with clearing life traumas, frustrations and anxieties, balancing our focus and awareness; has a stabilising effect on our disposition with others.

Rhodochrosite   Stone for lovers, expanding inner joy and honesty in relationships.

Rhodonite   A very vibrant pink with red through it, Rhodonite works with self love, opening your heart centre to self love.

Rose quartz   A very beautiful pink colour. It works very well with love, especially in the relationship between mother and child. It is a very loving crystal to give to children.

Ruby   Works very well with expanding the heart centre and keeping our physical health in balance.

Smoky quartz   This helps us to see our problems and opens them up to us. It extends our awareness so that we see our problems for what they really are.

Tiger's-eye   Traditionally used to protect us from the evil eye or the negativity of others. When worn in a situation where others are confronting us this stone will assist us by showing others our truth and an awareness of our honesty and good will.

Topaz   Works with stimulating the endocrine system; stimulates and aids in digestion, beneficial to the intake of nutrients.

Tourmaline   Assists with weight reduction and general balance in the endocrine system. It earths our awareness, which stops us from becoming vague and confused.

Turquoise   Works with protection. It keeps us protected from our enemies and from negative influences that exist around us. It is excellent for communication and opening the throat. It gives us strength when we need to uphold our beliefs and truths against confrontation.

Variscite   Calming and balancing, cleansing the environment we exist in, assists with food digestion and general health balance.

The dream influences of crystals

Crystals can be programmed with affirmations, our dreams and desires and actually stimulate our subconscious into recognising our requests. Through programming, a crystal that relates to us while we are asleep can also stimulate the reality in our awakened state.

Have the crystal as close to you as possible for dreaming—on the nightstand, under your bed, or under your pillow. The programming process is the same for most crystals; I will mention any deviations as we proceed.

Adventurine   Green in colour, adventurine is a variety of quartz. It works on extending our awareness and focus. Wonderful to work with in meditation because it allows us to step out of our physical life and go on a journey of freedom and relaxation so that we come back from meditation very refreshed. The same applies with our sleep state.

Adventurine allows us to disconnect from our everyday thought pattern and have a restful period of sleep. It stimulates a relaxation through the whole of our body so that we awaken feeling much more in balance. No programming necessary.

Agate   Normally sold in plate form or thin slices, agate can be highly polished and comes in a range of colours from browns and oranges through to reds, blues and greens. While you are asleep agate emits a balance throughout the chakra centres very similar to amethyst in its effects, except that it works with the acceptance of what is real and what is fantasy in your dream state. No programming necessary.

Alexandrite   From the chrysoberyl family, blue in colour. While we are asleep it expands and opens our potential awareness of what we need to let go of in our lives. It shows us where we are being stubborn and refusing to look at circumstances for what they really are. It opens us to clarity and awareness of ourselves. It assists us to discover and release restrictions and blocks in our life during sleep. No programming necessary.

Amber   The colouring comes in variations of gold, orange and yellow. Amber can be sold in different forms and shapes such as polished fossilised pieces and beads. Amber works wonderfully with us during our sleep state to assist us in letting go of feelings of being hurt. Where there has been an argument, a disagreement, amber is a wonderful stone to use to help us clear and remove the effect of other people on us. It soothes us and allows us to give self love and balance. Amber opens us to divine love and while we are asleep it can aid us in becoming closer in our awareness to the Creator—our God focus. It can bring us into harmony with our own life philosophy and an acceptance of who we are and what we believe in life. It is helpful in meditation as it allows us to integrate, understand and accept that which we awaken in our self-discovery through meditation or sleep. No programming necessary.

Amethyst Purple in colour. Takes on many shapes, including what we call geodes, which are the 'egg' of the amethyst broken open to show tooth-like structures. They can also be purchased in single structures called terminators with either one point or two. Amethyst also comes in pebble-like pieces. It should be programmed with your desires, as described on page 121; it will also respond on its own to balance and align your body while you are sleeping. It works on cleansing the aura, promoting peace and harmony, health and well-being.

Aquamarine A vibrant stone from the beryl family. It works on replenishing clarity of mind and aids in expanding our creative awareness so that while we are asleep we can actually come up with some excellent ideas that we want to put into practice in our everyday life. It stimulates concepts and ideas that we can trigger and relate to at a later date. It allows us extended vision so that we are seeing situations or circumstances in a broader view. Through this we can actually digest and clear up our problems while we are asleep. If this stone is close to us it will help us recognise the clarity and understanding that we need. It also works well with meditation to help us work through whatever crisis we're in at that time and acceptance of our positive qualities. We gain more confidence in ourselves by what we see in ourselves with this stone's assistance. No programming necessary.

Azurite A fairly rare crystal that is found in deep blue shades and so is quite valuable when cut and polished. Used in meditation or close to you in sleep it gives the facility to see everything in the meditative focus in a clear precise manner. It cuts through delusion or uncertainty. It lifts the veil in our awareness and allows us to see things clearly and precisely. It helps us go through our transformation of change and balance in ourselves, in our creativity, in our intuitive awareness. It allows progressive growth and change in ourselves. No programming necessary.

Bloodstone Reddish orange in colouring, works well on healing the body while we are in deep sleep and on detraumatising the system. All the exhaustion and tiredness from the day's activities take us into a deeper state of sleep where the bloodstone works on re-balancing and clearing out the extremes of the day. It brings us back into balance with ourselves so that we awaken feeling refreshed and ready to attack the world again. No programming necessary.

Calcite A hexagonal crystal that is usually opaque or translucent white. It works with inner peace and harmony and actually clears out hyperactivity. If we are over-active when we are going to sleep this would be the stone to have close by because it helps release the extended energy that is present and brings one back into self-balance so that we can sleep and wake feeling refreshed. No programming necessary.

Carnelian Normally found in hues of orange, brown and red, carnelian works by helping us get in touch with ourselves and helping us unfold our awareness, self-discovery, and bringing that back into our physical awareness. Having the stone close to us during our sleep state would give us more insight into ourselves. No programming necessary.

Chrysocolla Green chunks—no programming needed. Works with healing the body. Good to have near the bed if you are very tired or recovering from an illness.

Chrysoprase Green chunks—no programming needed. Works on forgiveness. Helps clear anger. Good to give somebody else if you want them to forgive you.

Citrine A honey-gold to yellow colouring. A good stone to have next to you when you are going to bed if your body is in shock or trauma, if you suffer from arthritis, a blood disorder or any form of impurity through your body. It works on revitalising your system so it can actually help release the pain, tension or stress that you have built up in the day during your sleep hours. No programming necessary.

Clear quartz Clear or translucent, quartz is often ground and polished into various shapes (most common is the crystal ball). Its natural shape is the pillar and the single point is called a terminator. The point is where the crystal's energy emanates. Clear quartz needs to be programmed; it works with clarity and achievement. It magnifies what the individual is feeling. Feeling success? It will bring it to you. Go to bed affirming you have already achieved what you are focusing on at the moment: the crystal will assist in bringing it toward you.

A clear crystal with green 'moss' inside it attracts fertility, money and prosperity. Needs to be programmed.

Diamond   Very valuable to have near you prior to sleep as they help sustain, calm and balance you while you are asleep. They help your spirit align in the astral and bring back clarity and recall of your astral projection. They also clear memory and you awaken feeling refreshed and revitalised.

Emerald   Green in colour, beneficial to have close to us while sleeping as it expands our spiritual insight and allows us to explore love, tranquility, balance, healing and even our own potential patience. It works with emotional balancing and harmony and brings us back from sleep feeling more secure and in harmony with ourselves and the world around us. No programming necessary.

Fluorite   Takes many shapes; the most popular and best for programming is the octahedron which is the shape the crystal forms when fully grown. Colour ranges through milky white, to blue-green and yellow, to a range of purples and violets. All are beneficial to dreaming—your choice. This is a lovely crystal to program for our dreams and goals, for the achievements we would like to create, the opportunities we want to open up for us in our lives. This stone is most valuable in helping us remember our dreams but assists us in understanding and can also open us to past-life recall.

Garnet   Red, small polished pebbles—no programming needed. Works on healing the heart, taking your dream space back to past-life recall. An uplifting stone promoting vitality; helps you awaken feeling refreshed.

Jade   Normally found in shades of green, jade is a stone that works well on inner peace and balance. It makes us very clear on activities in life where we are wrong or right. It is a judgment stone and helps us recognise the truth about whatever we are perceiving in life. (Probably why you see so much jade in Chinese architecture and decoration, even from ancient times.) No programming necessary.

Kunzite   A whitish stone with a pink tinge, powerful in opening the heart centre and helping us to connect with our own spiritual awareness. It works with tolerance and acceptance of others; compassion is a feeling and emotion we explore while working closely with this stone. Kunzite helps work with our own creative expression and expands our communication skills, particularly with other people. No programming necessary.

Lapis lazuli   Blue in colour, sold as a small stone or chunk, usually polished. It is the stone that works on the inner sanctuary of the human being, making us feel safe and secure. It does not need programming, it just emanates a feeling of calmness. Dream recall is also activated.

Malachite   Small pieces or chunks, green in colour. This is a stone that relates to the heart and if near your bed at night will help you deal with matters of the heart, problems with loved ones, clearing of anger and hurt. Works with awakening our own self-imposed limitations and blocks, and helps us accept release and deal with them. No programming necessary.

Moldavite   A deep green colour. Positive in meditation because it gives us concentration and focus. It allows us to explore levels and dimensions beyond our physical. In association with the sleep state it helps us go back into past-life recall, bringing up memories from other life experiences. No programming necessary.

Moonstone   Normally sold in small pieces or jewellery. This is the stone to clear melancholy, wonderful to have near us for our sleep times. If we are depressed or sad it will help us open up our dreams to release our emotions and awake feeling more in tune with ourselves. It gives us more flexibility in our attitudes and aligns us with all levels of ourselves. Dream recall is also activated. Once again no programming is necessary.

Peridot   Usually found in lighter green shades. Stimulates your inner consciousness and what you would like to change or activate in your life. Having it close to your bedside will activate and allow you an awareness of new ideas and fresh concepts that you feel very confident about in your awakened state. It helps you with activating change and growth in your physical life.

Pyrite   Fool's gold. Metallic shades of dark yellow/brown. Enhances our inner emotional feelings and brings us into harmony with ourselves and others. It is a great stone to work with if we're having relationship problems as it helps gain understanding and clarity to resolve whatever conflicts are being dealt with.

Rhodochrosite   Usually rose red in colour. Sold in small pebble-like stones, thin strips or chunks. A stone of self-love; relates to children and adolescents.

It does not need to be programmed and once again emanates a feeling of inner tranquility. Rhodochrosite will help our children accept themselves and become more comfortable with who they are. It helps extend our awareness of what we call divine love, an acceptance of self and life generally and all that is in tune with it.

Rhodonite Very similar to rhodochrosite, coming from the same family. It relays inner tranquillity for the adult person. It can help us confront issues about ourselves, to look at how others see us. It also helps with our understanding of inner strength and vulnerability, gives attunement with self and is an excellent stone for someone who works with people, as it helps detraumatise and clear out all that one's taken on belonging to others.

Rose quartz Crystal, but in slab form or chunks. Excellent for a child's room. It actually has an effect on our human vibration and therefore there is no need to manually program it—just place it near your bed and let it do the work itself. Rose quartz works on promoting love and harmony between mother and child; it promotes peace and a feeling of well-being, love and security. In an adult's room it promotes harmony and balance and will relay the love feeling across from husband to wife to make their sleep period more harmonious together.

Ruby Red in colour; works with inner strength, courage and determination. It also makes us aware of when we are at fault or when someone else is, so it gives us greater insight into our feelings and emotions and those of others. It stimulates love and passion. No programming necessary.

Smoky quartz Small chunks may be shaped into any form you want. Works with clearing deep-seated fears and restrictions and helps confront problems. This is a very popular crystal. No programming is necessary, but it can be programmed for other purposes, just like the clear quartz.

Tiger's-eye Bands of brown and black. Helps us recognise our inner stubbornness and refusal to see things as they are. It helps clear out blockage in meditation and the sleep state. For a woman having difficulty accepting the male in her life this stone will help clear out restrictions and allow the expansion and acceptance of a partner or potential lover to come into her life. No programming necessary.

Topaz White to gold to green. Does not need to be programmed as it emits and creates a wonderful environment for dreaming. It helps you in remembering your dreams and gives a great deal of balance during sleep. Helps one awaken feeling refreshed and revitalised.

Tourmaline Pillar crystals, hexagonal. Colour green to watermelon. Dream recall is activated. Works on revitalising energy to the physical body and does not need programming.

Turquoise Blue in colour. Sold in chunks. Does not need programming and once again will release your fears and uncertainties and help with balanced sleep.

Variscite A member of the turquoise family. Green in colour, it is usually sold in small pieces or chunks. It does not need programming. It emits a feeling of security and will help release fears and uncertainty.

APPENDIX C

Chakra Centres

The chakra centres were outlined in the section on the auric field in Chapter 1 (pages 19–23). They are discussed more fully here.

The aura or energy field surrounding the body has seven major focal points within the body called 'chakras', which work with the soul or life force. The chakra centres are the focal point of incoming and outgoing energy. They also provide long-term storage of data from this life as well as from past lives. Evidence for this theory is extensive, documented through hypnotic past-life regression and the reincarnation of recently departed souls who reappear as 'child geniuses', playing symphonies on the piano at the age of six, or quoting complex mathematical equations at far too young an age to have learned such things in this lifetime.

The seven chakra centres play a very big role in past-life recall because within them lie file storage, memory and the facility to reactivate past files. The chakra centres constantly receive data from the universal fohatic pool and store it to create the fohatic pool within you. The inner pool within the self, the storage place of all the data of your current life-experience, extends back through the chakra centres, through the astral bodies and eventually back to the universal fohatic pool. There is a continuous relay between the universal pool and the individual fohatic pool.

Seed-pods (*see* Glossary, p.145) containing the life experiences you choose to work with are stored within the fohatic pool, leading into the chakra centres to be released at an appropriate time in your life. Mid-life crisis is an example of a seed-pod 'eruption', in which you go through a crisis in your identity. You have the tools to help you through it if you can reach your past-life memory, feelings and emotions, so you can clear out and understand your own mortality. In your mid-life crisis you are looking at your descent towards mortality and at the years you have left, back at what you have achieved in your life so far, and forward at what you hope to achieve with the rest of your life. It is a time

The chakra centres

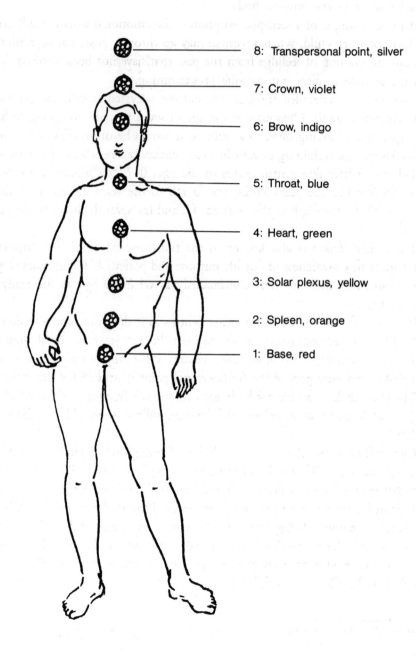

8: Transpersonal point, silver

7: Crown, violet

6: Brow, indigo

5: Throat, blue

4: Heart, green

3: Solar plexus, yellow

2: Spleen, orange

1: Base, red

of great introspection as you evaluate the purpose and meaning of life, and usually causes trauma to the physical body.

Another example of a seed-pod eruption is the emotional situation following the birth of a first child, when a woman may go through postnatal depression—perhaps an eruption of feelings from the past that have not been resolved. This is a prime time to clear out past-life programming.

Seed-pods are scheduled through life and are activated at different points in your physical growth. Obviously at the age of seven you are not going to have the experience of giving birth to a child, as it would be of no relevance to you.

Looking at the unfolding of your life, each chakra centre relates to a seven-year period: the first chakra centre relates to the ages 0–7; the second to the years 7–14, the third to the years 14–21, the fourth to the years 21–28, the fifth to the years 28–35, the sixth to the years 35–42, and the seventh chakra to the years 42 on.

The eighth chakra is also known as the transpersonal point. Its purpose is to integrate new awareness of our life purpose and potential. It continues to put new information into our lives continuously at whatever age we are ready or able to digest it.

It is slightly different from the other centres as it does not have a seven-year cycle. The transpersonal point has always been there to serve as a focal point for energy/data coming into the other chakra centres. It has only recently begun service as a chakra and only part of the transpersonal point is utilised for this purpose.

The seven chakras within the body each vibrate at a frequency which coincides with what humans see as colour (red, orange, yellow, green, blue, indigo and violet).[1]

Each chakra centre relates to a stimulation of energy and vitality in our bodies; they also store past-life recall and memory, as well as current life issues, issues that perhaps we have not dealt with and that will need our attention at a later date. Stored memory and its retrieval can occur through dream focus, while we are asleep a memory being activated through a particular chakra centre. The subconscious is the connection between chakra storage and the active brain. Each centre is associated with particular energy levels or issues that only that chakra can deal with. They are as follows:

---

[1] On 26 July 1992 there was an energy shift on the planet. One of the things that happened was the creation and recognition of the eighth chakra, located at the transpersonal point, about 30 cm/1 foot above the head. The colour ascribed to this centre is silver.

Base level or first chakra—red
Physical restrictions in life

This is where we stimulate all those physical restrictions that we have not worked with during our awakened state. In other words, where we have failed on a physical level and been unable to complete a task, perform up to expectations, either someone else's or our own. While we are asleep we would bring this up in our memory recall and it would activate as a dream.

All our feelings and inhibitions would show up in the dream, which would be trying to show us, in a re-enactment, how they are stopping us from succeeding. For example, we are trying to learn the computer and feeling as if we can't type and we are incompetent. We are programming ourselves here to be a failure at what we want to learn. Our mind is preoccupied with the belief that we are going to fail, which then becomes a reality.

Your employer may say, 'You're not paying any attention to what you're doing.' That can be very difficult to understand, because you are sitting there trying desperately to focus on what it is you have to learn. Unfortunately your subconscious fear of failure is fighting with what you're being taught.

Splenic level or second chakra—orange
Trauma, shock, recall

The left hemisphere of our brain is the area ascribed to logical thought and questioning while we are asleep. If you have been through some trauma which you have not resolved properly, a car accident which injured your neck, for the rest of your life, whenever the neck plays up you will get a reminder from the splenic level. For example, you see yourself in a state of fear or shock, reliving the memory of the accident, until you resolve the trauma.

Another activation might date back to you as a small child overhearing a very large argument between your parents who subsequently separated. You grow up, you marry, and one day have a very large argument with your spouse. At the splenic level you may bring up a dream of fear relating to the relationship, and activate unrealistic expectations. You may start to dream about your partner being with someone else, or even deserting you. This is very significant of the subconscious trying to say, 'You have fears and uncertainties about the relationship', which comes up from your memory of past experience. Your subconscious is trying to help you look at the experience as well as bring up your feelings and the deep subconscious fears that perhaps you're not looking at. This can have a very big effect on your life because obviously if you start dreaming about your partner being with someone else, you can start creating a belief that it is going to happen.

To give another example—perhaps you were in a duel with a person in a past life and you were murdered by him. Your subconscious can bring up a warning at the splenic level that you are making contact with that person again, giving you the opportunity to deal with the situation differently this time around. Not that the same situation would occur, but the fact that you have had a past problem with this person may cloud your vision on the actual potential of the relationship in this lifetime. Taking notice of your dream allows you to look at this person in a different way, without prejudice.

If the past life in which you were murdered was over one hundred years ago, you might well expect that duels of one sort or another were the accepted way of settling an argument. Today we are a bit less barbaric and diplomacy has become the order of the day, so we usually try to discuss a problem and resolve it without bloodshed or violence. In many instances this can result in the two people becoming very close friends after the misunderstanding is cleared up. Karma does follow us from lifetime to lifetime and so do the same people. We are given opportunity after opportunity to get it right and most of us finally will, after hundreds of thousands of lifetimes.

Solar plexus level or third chakra—yellow
Subconscious thoughts

At this third level we wrestle with ourselves daily, about what we are doing, what we think and what we feel about everything—from the weather to work-related areas, our personal life, people, things and places. Here we reawaken perhaps the strongest dream focus because this is where we subconsciously deal with things on a day-to-day basis. This is the level that we are normally dreaming from; whatever we are going through as a current issue is normally brought up to be looked at. If we have a situation occurring today that we are disturbed about—whether we should leave our job, make a date with someone who has phoned us, invest our money or spend it—when we go to sleep we actually bring up an awareness of our indecision and we wrestle with it throughout the night in our dream focus. We also do a positive association with past situations, so anything

that has been an issue that we have been trying to work with for many years
will continually come up through the subconscious focus, which is the yellow
frequency.

Again, we can reactivate anything that hasn't been resolved, perhaps a
relationship with an in-law whom we've had a problem with for twenty years.
Whenever a new problem arises with the inlaw, when we are asleep the
subconscious brings back a memory of this being a continuous problem for the
past twenty years. The dream then amplifies the problem; it may manifest in
this case with the person being killed or murdered or dying. On a conscious
level, of course, this awakens a lot of fear and we think, 'goodness me, I am
thinking bad thoughts of this person and look what is happening.' That person
may, in fact, be very ill, but in reality it is just our subconscious trying to deal
with our inability to resolve an ongoing problem.

At this level past-life memories of issues we haven't worked with in other
life experiences come up and focus. Our karmic lesson in life is perhaps most
exposed to us at the solar plexus level of dreaming.

Past-life recall at this level works on where we failed ourselves or didn't succeed
with something we wanted to extend ourselves with. It is trying to show us
how we can reach beyond a point that we existed at before, and that we have
a lot more potential this time around, by bringing up memory of skills we have
had in the past.

Heart level or fourth chakra—green
Empathy and emotions

Here we feel and experience empathy and the sensations of emotion. The green
level activates our dream focus when we are in love, especially on love in the
early stages when our focus is on the person that we are attracted to, involved
with, marrying. It also relates to any pain that we have been dealing with; we
can activate very abstract dreams at this level because at times we are out of touch
with our feelings and it is hard to explain how we feel in some instances. As
a result the dream can become extremely abstract in what it shows you.

Perhaps the pain is that we're still dealing with the loss of a loved one; we
have a dream where we see the loved one going away from us. Within the dream
we get symbolic focuses of flowers or jewellery, pearls or diamonds, which are
very significant of tears, emotions and clarity of feelings. Here the subconscious
is trying to get us in touch with our feelings and what we are not dealing with.

Here we also bring up past-life recall relating to associations with people who were around us. When we make contact in this lifetime with someone we have experienced some form of a relationship with in the past life we start dreaming about them—this is stimulated from this heart level.

Throat level or fifth chakra—blue
Communication

When we are having difficulty expressing our thoughts to another person, perhaps in a position where we are feeling as if somebody is speaking over us and we can't get our opinion across, or generally say what we feel or think, our dream state would be amplifying the problem, at the blue level, showing us chasing after people, trying to get their attention or making a show of ourselves where people stop and look at us. This is normally making the point that we have difficulty with communication.

When we are successful with our communication (people are patting us on the back and we are getting a lot of verbal acceptance and approval) the dream would go into a form where we might see ourselves as a royal person or attaining great wealth in the things we desire in our dream space. This is the subconscious amplifying that our ego has been placated, that we are feeling very good about who we are, that we are in touch with our confidence and self-awareness.

The blue level would also amplify if we were affected by someone else's communication, suddenly feeling very haunted by what they said or what they did or their general mannerisms. Here again the past-life recall would be on a past association or connection where a person's verbal communication had a great affect on us, and perhaps this was that person.

Brow level or sixth chakra—indigo
Higher level of consciousness

At this level we bring up all our past-life recall. It is also where we work with the intellectual mind, where we are opening up our creativity and extending awareness. It is where we gain ideas and concepts that we are going to work with, and this is the type of dream we have. When we wake up in the morning and feel that we have just resolved that project at work or the problem that we had with particular ideas or direction, the answers have been coming to us in our sleep. This is the level that we do it at. We also resolve and work with our own fertility at this level, as it works with our pituitary gland and family structure, developing and creating what we really want in life.

The indigo level also goes back to past-life memories of all sorts of life experiences; it opens us up to the pool of memory to give us a great deal of confidence and help with direction. We are continually bringing up an awareness of our capabilities in our dream space at this level.

Crown level or seventh chakra—violet
God and creation concept

At this level we have acceptance of who we really are. It is where we wrestle with ourselves about exactly who we are and what we are doing with our life. We bring up a lot of recognition of past associations; it is where we put the past side by side with the present in our dream state, and look at them objectively.

The transpersonal point or eighth chakra—white/silver

The colour of the transpersonal point is white through to silver. The white level of colour vibration works with the transpersonal point as the receiver of information and data, which it relays through into the seven major chakra centres.

The silver level, which is the eighth chakra, the higher vibrational level of white, disperses the integration of new data to the appropriate lower chakras. We could call it the eruption of new consciousness in the physical plane. It relates to the integration of our broader understanding and increased sensitivity relating to where we exist and what is going on for us on this planet and in its evolutionary cycle.

It also relates to constantly evolving humanity becoming more sensitised to their own sensations and working with their hypersensitivity. This means we are now instinctively working with our sixth sense, whether we like it or not.

For some of us human beings this means having a great deal of difficulty just being sensitive, as we are now having to look at the realities of life more than we ever have before. This brings us to an awareness of what control we have over our own lives and growth, and the life and growth of the planet and its evolution

The frustration with this difficulty is likely to manifest initially as anger and negativity on a personal level, perhaps even a community level.

In summary, we are continually activating dreams at all the different levels of our chakras, depending on what our life experience is at the moment. Some areas are more dominant than others. We may go through a period where we have a sequence of a particular type of dream which relates to the yellow level, the solar plexus, where we are having a lot of difficulties in life. Even without realising it we do listen to our dreams and take notice of what is coming up in them. We may not understand them at the time, but in our daily awakened state our dreams influence the decisions that we make. We really are talking to ourselves while we are asleep.

We may have a major focus on the solar plexus level while we are working through a collection of crises and then perhaps move on to the heart level, with a new relationship or stimulation and expansion of a relationship that we are in. Parenthood is well expressed at the green level, and at the solar plexus level, because we are dealing with responsibility as well as love and harmony. Then we may move on to the blue level where we are working with communicating with our children and trying to help them with their own development and positive outlook on life.

Glossary

Akashic records (also known as the *fohatic pool* or *fohatic energy field*) The memory of all life experience that is stored in the astral levels (fourth dimension); the collective memory of all living beings once they physically die; the memory of the entirety of a being's life is stored in the Akashic records. Like a computer it contains the discs of all memory. (*See* fohatic pool)

Astral plane We exist in the physical plane as human beings. When we die we exist in another dimension of understanding called the astral plane. We exist in the astral when we do not have a physical body but instead are a spirit or soul. There are seven levels or sub-planes within the astral.

Astral body (sometimes referred to as *celestial bodies*) These are energy deposits of the memories from past lives and other data taken from the fohatic pool and deposited along the astral plane during our descent into life, to be used when it becomes appropriate. The counterpart to our physical body which exists in the astral plane, the astral body is the receiver of information from our soul of our life experience and relays memory to us through our chakra centres. It exists while we are physical and when we die it retrieves all the information of our life experience and collectively stores it in the fohatic pool or Akashic records.

Aura The aura is a measurable electric energy field surrounding the body. It radiates a bright colour around our body which to the adept appears as a beautiful rainbow.

Cellular memory That memory that is brought forward at the cell level from past lives and stored in our chakra centres to be retrieved throughout life as life experience triggers the need.

Chakras The seven primary energy centres in the body. The aura relays information from the fohatic pool or Akashic records through to the astral bodies then through into our physical awareness through our chakra centres. They radiate the energy of life—they are the connection points for physical/spiritual being that we are; they assist our physical body in retaining its health and well-being through their natural breathing or cleansing process, which is actively happening throughout the cycle of our lives.

Clairvoyance ('clear vision') This is the ability to perceive the aura and to communicate with guides who help interpret the aura.

Devas or devic spirit (also known as *elementals*) Nature spirits that work with the natural elements: Earth, Wind, Fire, Water and Wood (the fifth element is sometimes listed as Ether instead of Wood, depending on whose book you are reading). These spirits assist with the management of our environment.

Etheric body (the 'soul') This is a perfect duplicate of the physical body but with no mind as we know it. It is like a battery for the physical body. Without the etheric body and its transference of prana (vital life force) into the physical body, we're dead. This vital life force permeates every cell of the etheric body, and therefore, the physical body. Within the etheric body is the 'tree of life', the trunk being the etheric spinal cord, and the branches the etheric nerves. These are the etheric counterparts of the nerves found in the physical body. For every physical organ there is an etheric counterpart, hence when someone loses a leg, for instance, the leg sensation continues. The etheric body must at all times be properly attuned to the dense physical for perfect health to be manifest.

Fohatic pool (also known as the *fohatic energy field* or *Akashic records*) The archives in the fourth dimension of all universal knowledge encompassing every thought and every deed that has ever been or ever will be. The pool of experiential consciousness in the physical form which is the information stored in the human aura.

Guides Spirits that exist in the astral planes who can communicate with us in the physical plane to help us throughout our lives with understanding.

Higher self (also see *over-soul*) The highest level of guidance in the astral who is considered to be another part of ourselves. Our ultimate teacher who guides and shines a light on our awareness and understanding of our own life purpose. (Can also be called a guardian angel.)

Karma (karmic law)   The penalty or reward incurred as a result or consequence of past action from this or another lifetime.

Karmic blueprint   The blueprint that we come into life with, programmed with the potential of what we can create in life, like a life-map with potential coordinates. The experiences we 'must' have and the experiences we 'may' have.

Lesson   What we came into this life to learn and/or the karma we must work through.

Meditation   Quieting the mind to achieve single-minded thought.

NREM   Non Rapid Eye Movement, the deeper levels of non-dreaming sleep known as theta and delta.

Out-of-body   An out-of-body experience occurs when your spirit takes a break from your body and travels into the astral plane to meet other spirits. Time does not exist in the astral so we may have experiences in the past or in the future. We may re-live part of a past life to resolve unfinished issues, we may meet someone to work on a current issue, or we may travel into the future to lay the groundwork for something which is going to occur in our present life.

Over-soul   A community of individual spirits who are capable of working separately but choose to work as one mind. They are synergetic or co-habitant spirits existing as a unified civilisation. Any cellular part of the over-soul expressing as an individual form or extended consciousness is recognised as the higher self of an individual physical being.

Parallel life structure   Another person who exists in our time or another period (past-life connection) who has an effect on our lives (and vice versa) through a karmic association with us in the astral planes. Through this association we are striving to experience similar understanding. (Also called a *parallel twin soul*.)

Past life   A time gone by when our soul inhabited another physical body. Our experiences of that life have been recorded in the fohatic pool or Akashic records. Past-life recall in the dream state is an out-of-body experience, but only in the past. It is stepping back into the past to re-experience the sensations, feelings and understandings of the past in order to clear up an unresolved issue or gain a better understanding of a situation similar to one we are currently working on.

Pre-birth Council   The body of spirits that work with our map of life, the potential life-path that we will utilise through the innate awareness of life direction from the memory that is given us for our journey in the physical.

Precognition   Knowing in advance that a situation will occur. Recognition of a future event. (Also called *déjà vu*.)

REM   Rapid Eye Movement, occurring in the lighter stages of sleep (characterised by alpha brain waves), a stage of sleep in which dreaming occurs at roughly 90-minute intervals.

Seed-pods   Time-released life experiences, as established by the blueprint, that are necessary for growth and understanding.

Spirit guide   A being that exists in the astral plane, a spirit which elects to offer its services to guide us in our life.

Snakes or serpents   A snake is seen as the commonly known reptile while the serpent is significantly larger, sometimes mythical or mystical in nature, and may have the ability to talk as the serpent spoke to Eve in the Garden of Eden.

Twin soul   Another part of us. Two parts of the same, atomistically split to form two individual people on the physical plane—when we die we become one memory.

Dream workbook

Use these pages as a guide to setting out your own dream workbook.

Date: . . . .

Dream:

. . . .

. . . .

. . . .

. . . .

. . . .

. . . .

. . . .

. . . .

. . . .

Symbols:

. . . .

. . . .

Awakened day:

Clothes worn:

. . . .

. . . .

Events:

....

....

....

....

....

....

....

....

....

....

Comments:

....

....

....

....

....

....

....

....

Watch for tonight's dream or one within a few days to reflect something concerning any unresolved personal conflicts.

Date: ....

Dream:

....
....
....
....
....
....
....
....
....
....
....
....

Symbols:

....
....

Awakened day:

Clothes worn:

....
....

Events:

....

....

....

....

....

....

....

....

....

Comments:

....

....

....

....

....

....

....

....

....

....

Watch for tonight's dream or one within a few days to reflect something concerning any unresolved personal conflicts.

Bibliography

Atkinson, Atkinson, Smith, Hilgard, *Introduction to Psychology*, 9th edition. New York: HBJ College Publications, 1987

Bailey, A.A. *Discipleship in the New Age*, Vol 1, 1944. Reprint. New York: Lucis Publishing Company, 1976

—— *Discipleship in the New Age*, Vol 2, 1955. Reprint. New York: Lucis Publishing Company, 1972

—— *Esoteric Astrology*, 1951. Reprint. New York: Lucis Publishing Company, 1979

—— *Esoteric Healing*, 1953. Reprint. New York: Lucis Publishing Company, 1977

—— *Esoteric Psychology*, vol. 1, 1936. Reprint. New York: Lucis Publishing Company, 1975

—— *Esoteric Psychology*, vol. 2, 1942. Reprint. New York: Lucis Publishing Company, 1975

—— *Externalisation of the Hierarchy*, 1957. Reprint. New York: Lucis Publishing Company, 1976

—— *From Intellect to Intuition*, 1932. Reprint. New York: Lucis Publishing Company, 1974

—— *Glamour: A World Problem*, 1950. Reprint. New York: Lucis Publishing Company, 1971

—— *Initiation, Human and Solar*, 1922. Reprint. New York: Lucis Publishing Company, 1974

—— *Letters on Occult Meditation*, 1922. Reprint. New York: Lucis Publishing Company, 1974

—— *The Light of the Soul*, 1927. Reprint. New York: Lucis Publishing Company, 1978

—— *The Rays and the Initiations*, 1960. Reprint. New York: Lucis Publishing Company, 1976

—— *Telepathy and the Etheric Vehicle*, 1950. Reprint. New York: Lucis Publishing Company, 1975

—— *A Treatise on Cosmic Fire*, 1925. Reprint. New York: Lucis Publishing Company, 1977

—— *A Treatise on White Magic*, 1934. Reprint. New York: Lucis Publishing Company, 1974

Bendit, L.J. & P.D. *The Etheric Body of Man*, 1977. Reprint. Wheaton, Illinois: Theosophical Publishing House, 1977

Besant, A. *A Study in Consciousness*, 1904. Reprint. Adyar, India: Theosophical Publishing House, 1975

—— *Thought Power.* 1903. Reprint. Adyar, India: Theosophical Publishing House, 1969

Brennan, B.A. *Hands of Light*, New York: Bantam Books, 1988

—— *Function of the Human Energy Field in the Dynamic Process of Health, Health and Disease*, New York: Institute for the New Age, 1980

Cayce, Edgar. *Auras*, Virginia Beach, Virginia: ARE Press, 1945

Dworetzky, John P. *Psychology*, 2nd ed. St Paul, Minnesota: West Publishing Co.

Harrison, J. *Love Your Disease*, Sydney: Angus & Robertson, 1984

Hill, D. *Edge of Reality*, Sydney: Pan Books (Australia) Pty Ltd, 1987

—— *Reaching for the Other Side*, Sydney: Pan Books (Australia) Pty Ltd, 1982

Hodson, G. *The Kingdom of the Gods*, 1952. Reprint. Adyar, India: Theosophical Publishing House, 1970

Landsdowne, Z.F. *The Chakras and Esoteric Healing*, York Beach, Maine: Samuel Weiser Inc., 1987

Leadbeater, C.W. *The Chakras*, 1927. Reprint. Wheaton, Illinois: Theosophical Publishing House, 1977

—— *The Hidden Side of Things*, 1913. Reprint. Adyar, India: Theosophical Publishing House

—— *Man Visible and Invisible*, 1902. Reprint. Wheaton, Illinois: Theosophical Publishing House, 1977

—— *Telepathy and Mind-Cure*, London: Theosophical Publishing House, 1926

—— *A Textbook of Theosophy*, 1912. Reprint. Adyar, India: Theosophical Publishing House

Motoyama, Dr Hiroshi, *The Functional Relationship between Yoga Asanas and Acupuncture Meridians*, Tokyo: IARP, 1979

Ostrander, S. and Schroeder, L. *Psychic Discoveries Behind the Iron Curtain*, Englewood Cliffs, New Jersey: Prentice-Hall, 1970

Plotnik, R. & Mollenauer, S.: *Brain and Behaviour*, New York: Harper & Row, 1978

Powell, A.E. *The Astral Body*, 1927. Reprint. Wheaton, Illinois: Theosophical Publishing House, 1978

—— *The Causal Body and the Ego*, 1928. Reprint. Wheaton, Illinois: Theosophical Publishing House, 1978

—— *The Etheric Double*, 1925. Reprint. Wheaton, Illinois: Theosophical Publishing House, 1987

—— *The Mental Body*, 1927. Reprint. Wheaton, Illinois: Theosophical Publishing House, 1975

Wilde, S. *Affirmations*, Taos, New Mexico: White Dove International, 1987

Index